Behind the Scenes
with Hollywood
Producers

Behind the Scenes with Hollywood Producers

Interviews with 14 Top Film Creators

DUANE BYRGE

Foreword by Robert Osborne

McFarland & Company, Inc., Publishers
Jefferson, North Carolina

Also of interest:
Duane Byrge *and* Robert Milton Miller,
*The Screwball Comedy Films:
A History and Filmography, 1934–1942*
(McFarland, 1991, paperback 2001)

ISBN (print) 978-0-7864-7211-6
ISBN (ebook) 978-1-4766-2491-4

LIBRARY OF CONGRESS CATALOGUING DATA ARE AVAILABLE

British Library cataloguing data are available

Front cover: Clint Eastwood on the set of *Invictus,* 2009
(Photofest/Warner Bros. Pictures)

Printed in the United States of America

McFarland & Company, Inc., Publishers
  Box 611, Jefferson, North Carolina 28640
  www.mcfarlandpub.com

Table of Contents

Foreword by Robert Osborne

Whenever I'm asked what movie I'd want to have with me if I were shipwrecked on a desert island, I admit the truth: rather than any specific film, I'd much rather find Duane Byrge on any shore I happen to wash up on—for a number of reasons. I know what a witty, bright guy he is, which means he'd be great company. And since he knows everything about a subject that never fails to interest me—Hollywood and how it works, both now and in its colorful past—I'd be guaranteed the conversation on that island would never lag, and would certainly be more engaging than watching the same film over and over.

I've known Duane since we were both staff writers at the old *Hollywood Reporter*, in bygone days when the initials *THR* stood for a daily trade publication many considered essential reading for keeping up with the Hollywood scheme of things. He's a first-rate writer and one hell of an interviewer who asks interesting, fresh questions of his subjects.

That's one reason this book is as entertaining as it is informative. Another is his focus on producers—the people in the film business most of us know the least about. Actors act. Directors direct. Photographers photograph and editors edit. But producers are harder to define because there are so many different species among them.

David O. Selznick, the independent producer who thrived in the 1930s and 1940s with films such as *Gone with the Wind*, *Rebecca*, *Duel in the Sun* and *The Third Man*, was one of the hands-on producers who did everything. He found the material, hired the director, cast the film, kept an eagle eye on every aspect of production, and occasionally directed some scenes, sometimes rewriting them during filming. He also wrote daily memos both criticizing and encouraging their recipients, which drove everyone bananas. And he made great movies.

Arthur Freed, an MGM producer during the studio's glory days, turned out some of the finest Hollywood musicals ever created. His formula was to hire the best people possible in all departments and,

1

keeping a sharp eye on what they were accomplishing, stay out their way. The result was a canon of musicals unmatched in quality, such as *Meet Me in St. Louis, Easter Parade, An American in Paris, Show Boat, Singin' in the Rain, The Band Wagon* and *Gigi*. And this just scratches the surface of his credits.

There are producers who rarely visit a film set, others whose main contribution is raising money to make a movie. Others—like Hitchcock and Billy Wilder—were directors who took on the additional responsibilities of producing only to keep someone else from getting in their hair while they were busy crafting their masterpieces (and occasional failures).

In his book, Duane Byrge covers a wide spectrum of those who are currently active as producers, from widely recognizable names, such as Clint Eastwood and Alan Ladd Jr. to those who don't have marquee names but have made major contributions to film. Byrge gives their credits and asks great questions, including the most basic one—"What does a producer do?"—which brings forth an amazing variety of answers.

Through it all, interesting things come out, such as why Clint Eastwood has not made a western since his Academy Award-winning *Unforgiven* in 1992; how Taylor Hackford was able to get permission to use a Phil Collins song in his 1984 film *Against All Odds*; and what led Hackford to say that *An Officer and a Gentleman* (1982)—filmed on location in Washington State—revealed to him "the realities and ugliness of Hollywood."

It's all in this book, along with much more—a trove of information, courtesy of Duane Byrge.

Robert Osborne is the prime-time host of *Turner Classic Movies*.

Preface

In this book, we look at creative producers, as opposed to those given the credit for solely securing the financing of a motion picture. The producers interviewed here start with an idea, develop it, nurture it, and stick with it, through marketing and release. Along the way, from pre-production to completion, they function as crisis managers.

Producers don't act, don't write, don't compose, don't edit and don't direct: they make things happen. Chili Palmer, Elmore Leonard's character in *Get Shorty*, says: "I don't think a producer has to know much of anything." The correct statement would be: A producer has to know something about everything and learn new things and models all the time.

Producers are entrepreneurs. Each film is like a start-up, involving new challenges, technologies and financial realities. They appreciate all the aspects of filmmaking, though they usually aren't expert in any. Each movie enterprise is unique, and old ways of doing things do not necessarily apply. Through it all, these creative professionals make sense out of uncertainty and chaos.

It's the producer, not the director or the star, who accepts the Academy Award for Best Picture. The interviewees in this book include seven who have won Best Picture: Tony Bill, Clint Eastwood, Mark Johnson, Alan Ladd Jr., Arnold Kopelson, Fred Roos and Jim Wilson. While he was a fledgling filmmaker, Taylor Hackford won an Oscar for Best Short Film.

All of them started out when there were no producing programs in film schools, and Fred Roos is the only one who set out to be a producer. While a student at UCLA in the 1960s, he determined that his best skill was recognizing talent and bringing it together. He kept his career goal to himself: in those rebellious times, the film school *cognoscenti* regarded producers as chain-wearing, cigar-smoking Philistines.

The producers interviewed here are an eclectic mix. Some are late '60s and early '70s college grads who didn't go into "plastics." They all were movie buffs before the age of Turner Classic Movies, DVDs and today's warp-speed, evolving modes of delivery. They come from a range of backgrounds. Some segued from other professions: Arnold Kopelson studied law, and Paula Wagner started as an actress.

All are self-starters: they deal with daily setbacks or reversals, but they keep their eyes on the prize. To be effective, they must initiate dialog, arrange meetings and sometimes get people to do things they don't want to do. They have to be deaf to the word "no," but not inflexible. Knowing when to move on from a project is a part of their longevity and success. Movie productions are time-consuming, and the secret is that they only work on things that they are passionate about. They must have stamina. Producing a movie is a marathon, and they know how to maintain their energies to go the distance.

Being a producer means meeting with potential investors, some of whom may be dilettantes who enjoy rubbing elbows in Hollywood circles but are not bottom-line serious about backing a movie. Thus producing a film involves a lot of wheel-spinning and side-stepping to get the project off the ground.

Once production starts, producing is, for the most part, crisis management. Producers must have superb communication skills. They must see the big picture and discern who needs to know what. They must be able to talk to a wide range of people with different talents and special skills. They must be pragmatic, diplomatic and, if necessary, emphatic.

When they are in production on a film, they are on the lookout for the next project. They thrive on creative multi-tasking, keeping numerous projects in various stages of development.

As the reader will learn, all share one trait: that first-timer enthusiasm for their latest project, like a kid with a new toy.

What makes them tick? What keeps them wound up, and why are they as passionate now as when they started out? In the following interviews, we'll see that, quite simply, a producer's work is never done—but then, none of them considers it work.

Marc Abraham

Marc Abraham is the head of Strike Entertainment, a development-production company he launched in 2002 in partnership with Thomas Bliss and Eric Newman. Strike has produced such fare as Alfonso Cuaron's futuristic Children of Men *(nominated for three Academy Awards),* Let's Go to Prison, *a dark comedy about prison life, and* Dawn of the Dead *and* The Rundown.

In 2008, Abraham made his directorial debut with Flash of Genius, *starring Greg Kinnear. Based on a true story, the film chronicles the life of a man who invented intermittent windshield wipers and takes on the Detroit automotive establishment to secure his patent claims. The picture won the prestigious Alfred P. Sloan Award and premiered at the Telluride Film Festival.*

In 1990, Abraham was a founding partner in Beacon Communications. Beacon produced such memorable films as director Alan Parker's The Commitments, *a comedy about a group of Irish singer-musicians who try to form a black blues band. It was nominated for a Golden Globe Award as Best Picture (Musical/Comedy) in 1992.*

Abraham spearheaded the formation of Beacon Records, which released the soundtrack to The Commitments *in association with MCA. The earthy R&B soundtrack sold more than two million copies. Overall, Beacon's five soundtracks sold more than four million units worldwide.*

Beacon also produced A Midnight Clear, *starring Ethan Hawke, and* A Thousand Acres, *based on the Pulitzer Prize–winning novel. During Beacon's successful run, Abraham's credits as a producer also include* Sugar Hill, *starring Wesley Snipes;* Princess Caraboo, *starring Phoebe Cates and Kevin Kline;* The Road to Wellville, *starring Anthony Hopkins;* The Baby-Sitters Club, *based on the Scholastic series of books;* The Family Man, *starring Nicolas Cage and Tea Leone;* Spy Game, *starring Robert Redford and Brad Pitt; and* Bring It On, *starring Kirsten Dunst and Gabrielle Union.*

Producer/director Marc Abraham behind the camera on *Flash of Genius* (2008). Courtesy of Marc Abraham.

He served as executive producer on the blockbuster Air Force One starring Harrison Ford and two sports-world films, The Hurricane, starring Denzel Washington, and For Love of the Game, starring Kevin Costner.

Abraham entered the film industry working on the documentary Playing to Win, an inside look at the Cuban athletic system. During the crew's often harrowing shoot in Havana, Abraham wrote the documentary's script.

Subsequently, he eked out a living in Los Angeles, writing spec screenplays and working freelance for the Santa Monica Evening Outlook. In addition, he wrote for the TV series 21 Jump Street and penned an episode of Moonlighting.

Abraham won a Writers Guild Award for The Earth Day Special in 1990. He serves on the board of the Virginia Film Festival, held every fall in Charlottesville, home to Abraham's alma mater, the University of Virginia.

Duane Byrge: You seem to thrive on multi-tasking.

Marc Abraham: I am preparing for a movie that I'm going to direct based on the life of Hank Williams, Sr., one of the most important American artists of the 20th century. His music influenced poetry. It influenced literature. It definitely influenced most of the important musicians that have come to put their mark on that period. Bob Dylan, Bruce Springsteen, Tom Petty, Neil Young—all of them point to Hank Williams as a seminal influence.

I've been working on this movie for five, six or seven years. It's had its ups and downs. I wrote the script, *I Saw the Light,* based on one of Hank's more famous songs. The writing was difficult but very satisfying.

In terms of making a music film, especially about a very famous person, one of the biggest impediments to getting the movie made, whether it's Bob Marley, Janis Joplin or Jimmy Hendrix, is getting the music. I spent a long time down in Nashville talking to the people who control the publishing rights, and Troy Tomlinson, who began originally working with the publisher to publish Hank's music.

Ultimately, they have been very supportive. They loved the idea of the movie. They loved the script. We've got the rights. I'm in the process of casting the movie. I've got an English actor, Tom Hiddleston, to play Hank. It looks like Amanda Seyfried is going to play his wife.

It will be financed by a company out of Vancouver. It is an independent film and is in the $10 million range. There is many a slip between the cup and the lip so you can never let up on something like that. You have to keep your eye on the ball every single day. To use a sports analogy: You move the ball one foot, one yard, one first down, and there are a lot of incomplete passes along the way.

So that's what I'm doing now. I'm also writing another script simultaneously, at night. It's one that I want to direct. I am also finishing up *RoboCop.*

Even with your productivity and energy level, you've described yourself as a reluctant producer.

When people ask me why I'm a producer, I always say "bad luck" because I never meant to become a producer. From the time I was in the fifth grade I used to write all the time. I wanted to be an artist. I was interested in writing novels, and I was interested in film. If I was going to do film, I thought I would be a writer and a director. The only thing I ever knew in those years about producers was what Raymond Chandler wrote in one of his detective mysteries. He had Philip Marlowe say that the only movie producers he knew had "the integrity of a slot machine."

When I got out of school, which was in the 1970s, people didn't worry about careers. I had a B.A. from the University of Virginia. I was never ever worried about what I was going to do. When I was at college I loved film, but there wasn't a film program at the University of Virginia. I went to every movie that was out. Those were the halcyon days of cinema, the '70s. Honestly, I bet if I came out now, it wouldn't appeal to me. What they're about now is making a lot of money.

But I was into the movies then, admiring guys like Hal Ashby. I remember driving to Richmond just to go to the opening of *Five Easy Pieces*. That was what I was excited about. Those kinds of movies were the movies I wanted to make.

I grew up in Louisville, Kentucky, and I knew I wasn't going to go back to Louisville. I knew I needed to see the footlights. I went to New York. I didn't know anybody. First I got a job where I drove a linen truck in Brooklyn for some Mafia types. I ended up, because of some connections at Virginia, in advertising.

I applied at Young & Rubicam. I didn't know the name, but I knew they were at 285 Madison Avenue. I had longer hair and a mustache. I was living in a little tiny apartment on the Upper East Side, ten by ten. They offered me a job.

I rode my bike to work. I began working on Madison Avenue as a copywriter trainee, in what they called traffic in those days. That's basically kind of shuffling stuff around inside. But it was Madison Avenue, and they paid me $8,000 for the year. It was $666 a month after taxes.

There was a tavern around my corner called O'Brien's. Guys would go down there, and they'd have burgers, two Bloody Marys, light up a cigarette in the elevator. It was like *Mad Men*. So I did that for a while, for eight or nine months. The guy I worked for had accounts he didn't want to work on. The agency had big stuff—a campaign they were working on with Orson Welles. I got put on one of those accounts he didn't want.

I didn't know one thing about it. It was actually a company owned by Norton Simon. He would basically buy up companies, cut them down and then flip them. I would go into stores, and assess sewing patterns. That would be my job.

I asked a buddy of mine, a brilliant guy who was in Harvard Business School, to help me figure out what I wanted to do. We rolled up a big fat joint and we drove. During the drive I was going to figure out my life. We got all the way to Montauk. On the way, I had an epiphany...

On the Way to Montauk, it's like Saul.

Yes, on the way to Damascus. All we talked about on the way up was the money. Twenty thousand dollars was a lot at the time. My father was probably only making $25,000. I was making $8,000 at Young & Rubicam. All I was thinking about was that I could buy a new KLH stereo. I was getting to understand the lay of the social strata of New York. I knew what that money could do—a single guy. It was 1972 or '73. Those were good times.

On the way back—I don't think we were as high—I had an epiphany. I realized that Young & Rubicam is a corporate structure. For me to get where I would be making $20,000 a year and have more authority, would take four more years. So, I thought, "If I didn't take that job, why am I here?" Within a month, I quit. I just gave it up. The guys at Young & Rubicam said, "Don't leave. You can be a star." They liked me.

I had a real vision on my way back from Montauk—I could see my whole life. I thought I'd be very successful in the business. I would be a successful advertising guy. Money would come. I'd be making more and more and I wouldn't be able to give it up. I felt like I could see down the road, and that road felt like it would lead to Darien, Connecticut [an affluent, upscale community].

I had this fierce thing that I wasn't going to do it. I got back, and I remember calling my dad. I told him about the job offer, and his reaction was like it always was: "Why would they offer you that job?" Later, I called him back and said I wasn't going to do it.

Very Benjamin Braddock.

Exactly, but my dad was very cool about it. He said, "All right, son, don't do it."

I got in my car and headed out to Colorado with my girlfriend.

When I look back, I think: "What was I thinking?" I ski-bummed for a while. Then I came out here to Los Angeles with her. I decided I was going to get into show business and write novels on the side. I didn't know anybody. I got an apartment in North Hollywood. I got a job working as a waiter at the Old World restaurant on Sunset Blvd., across from Tower Records.

When I was in New York, I met the son of George Roy Hill. He was a carpenter who built my bunk bed in that tiny apartment. When I got out here, his father was "God." I called him while he was editing *Butch Cassidy*. He never took the call, but I had the illusion that I had a touchstone to the movie business.

I thought, "Well, maybe I'll become an actor. That will help me get into show business." I got an agent. I'd go to auditions. I went out on a few commercials things. I was terrible. It was humiliating. So, I worked during the day at Old World, and I got a job working at a ski shop at night in Brentwood.

While I was working at the ski place, I decided to write screenplays. I'd never written a screenplay in my life, but I got a couple of them, saw what they were. I learned the format.

For me, fundamentally, it's been an interesting road. I've had successes as a producer, but it wasn't really what I wanted to do. What happened is that I started writing. I wrote a bunch of movie scripts. Finally, I met Julia Phillips at a party.

How did you get into a party of that level?

I was running around then [*laughs*]. I was starting to have a social life. In those days, it was a lot of sex, drugs and rock 'n' roll, and I was down for all three. It was just such a looser time.

[Julia] had won an Academy Award for *The Sting*. She had done *Taxi Driver*. Julia had read a script of mine and kind of liked it. She had a deal she put together at Fox. She ended [up] sort of giving me a deal at Fox. It was a crazy time. I left out some interesting things there [*laughs*]. For a short time, I had an office on the lot. I thought, "Oh my God, this is insane."

That craziness got me in the door a little bit. But I was struggling to make a living. I was writing on the side. I was writing spec screenplays. I wanted to write books. I was writing sports. I got a job writing for a little golf magazine. Because of that, I met some people. Bruce Jenner had just won the decathlon at the Olympics. He wanted to do a book on how the negotiations for the Olympics went. It was sort of a guide to the Olympic games. They paid me ten grand. I was thrilled. I wrote that book in 1980. Bruce didn't write any of it. So, I had a book. Down the line I wrote another one on the next Olympics in 1984.

My screenplays were not getting sold. I wrote a book of motivational speeches. I would write anything for anybody who would pay me.

I was collecting unemployment, and I had discovered Santa Monica by then. Cathy Smith was very big with her exercising videos. I ghosted her first exercise book and got something like $7,000. I was writing a string of articles for the *Evening Outlook* in Santa Monica. I would cover boxing matches that were down at the Olympic Auditorium.

I was getting around and meeting all sorts of people. I kept trying to write, write. A friend of mine had directed *What's Love Got to Do with It*, and so I just kept pushing along. At that time, I met up with a French-German film crew, and they wanted to make a film about the Cuban athletic system, which was in those days subsidized by the Soviet Union. They needed somebody to write it. So in 1984 I signed on to write a documentary on the Cuban Athletic Association.

You couldn't get into Cuba, and I went in surreptitiously with a film crew through Mexico. When I got down there, they thought I was with the CIA. They kept me in my hotel room for two days.

Then they gave us access. They had a guy with us all the time. I spent three weeks in Cuba. It was really intense, and I got sick. I got ready to get out. It was an interesting experience. The documentary was called *Playing to Win*. I got to interview all these guys, Alberto Juantorena, the whole baseball team, and Teófilo Stevenson.

I came back, and I got some assignments. In the meantime, I hustled up a couple of jobs. I wrote an episode of *Moonlighting*. I got it because someone I knew gave me the shot. That was a big deal for me. I also had another friend who was working on a show called *21 Jump Street*, and I got a job writing two episodes. I wasn't really very good at it, but I was happy to do it.

Through my first wife, I met Armyan Bernstein. He was a big screenwriter at the time. He had written *One from the Heart* that Coppola did. He and I had talked about writing a script together. We had an idea about an eco-thriller, which in those days was not something that anybody was doing. We wrote this environmental thriller called *Crystal Clear*. They paid us like 250 grand.

You hit the jackpot. You were no longer eking out a freelance existence.

I got a big check. I was happy. Tom Cruise was attached to it. It took place in Kentucky. We met Tom there. That didn't work out [the film was never made] but we'd been paid.

Then Army [Bernstein] and I talked about doing another script together. We started pitching ideas around. Army knew a guy he went to school with in Wisconsin, who was living in Chicago. His name was Tom Rosenberg. He had a lot of money, and he wanted to start a little film company. So we had a meeting with Tom. He told us that he didn't care if he made a penny. He just wanted to invest.

We met a great guy, Ian La Fresnais. I was playing tennis with him one day. He had read the galleys of this book written by a British school-teacher named Roddy Doyle. He asked me if I wanted to read it. I said, "We've got this little company called Beacon Pictures, and we're trying to make these little films." So I read it and loved it. It was all about music, and I'd been around the music scene.

One of my best friends was living in Ireland. Alan Parker had been involved with the project. He was going to do *Les Miserables* for $30 million. They kept working on Alan, and we said [Beacon] would option the book. So we just cobbled together *The Commitments*. I don't want to take too much credit for that other than finding it. I didn't even get producer credit on it.

You were listed as co-producer, which is a creative credit.

True, but in the business end of it I brought that project into being. That's what I did, I nourished it. I was more the seed, but the man that made that movie was Alan Parker. He is a brilliant filmmaker with great taste and instincts.

Army was great. He did his thing. Through it all, I learned how to get a movie going. We had just started out, and all of a sudden, we had a winner on our hands.

The movie turned out to be great. The soundtrack, and my buddy, Mark Roswell—who I still work with—ended up putting together a 20-minute piece with Alan. We sold the music rights to Universal. Again, it was something I engineered. We sold it to Alan Keller at Universal. We got $900,000. Then the record sold four million copies. It made Beacon a lot of money.

Suddenly, I was a producer. The next thing I know, we tried to get the rights to *Midnight Clear*. It was a wonderful anti-war movie. Jon Levin of CAA first gave me the script, and we optioned it. We put it together with Peter Berg. It was Gary Sinise's first role. Frank Whalley was in it. People loved it. It's hard to find now, but it's a really good movie.

Pretty soon, we were figuring it out. Before I know it, we were into producing *Sugar Hill* with Wesley Snipes and then *Baby-Sitter's Club*.

We were making movies. That's how I became a movie producer. All my creative energy was getting pulled into it. I was slowly becoming better as a film producer. I put a lot of energy into the material. I was writing a lot of my ideas into the projects. I was putting all my creative energy into other people's stuff, which was fine. Sometimes [the projects weren't] that good.

Before I knew it, our success had driven us into a position where we were making movie after movie. Up until then, everything was just scraping by. Now we were starting to make money. Beacon was thriving. We made some good movies—*Hurricane, For Love of the Game.* Pretty soon my partner was doing his movies, and I was doing my movies.

How did your background in sports spur your producing Bring It On?

A woman who worked for me at the time, Caitlin Scanlon, found it. It was something called *Cheerleading*. It was a script that had all the basics of *Bring It On*. It was unpolished but that whole way they talked, all the jargon, all the lingo that was so big a part of the movie came from [writer Jessica Bendinger].

It was a lot of real work to get the script to where we needed it. But all scripts do. They all need that. Sometime it was a bumpy road. Caitlin had the vision on that. That was when we had a deal at Universal. Our first deal, when we made *The Commitments*, we had a deal with Fox because of Army's relationship with them. We made *Sugar Hill* for them.

With Beacon, we had a real good company. Then we moved to Sony, where we made what became our first giant movie, *Air Force One*. That was a good movie, with Wolfgang Petersen directing. That was the last movie we made in our deal there.

How did you get that?

Andrew Marlowe, a writer, came in with the idea for *Air Force One*. We developed it, and Army got involved. He helped land Harrison [Ford]. Very soon we were doing the movie.

I was going off to do a lot of movies—*Spy Game, Family Man*. During that time my partner and I had a parting of the ways. We sold the company to an international company, Comsat.

I still had a deal at Universal. I started Strike with Tom, and, basically, Gary was the number-three guy. Now we're partners. We did *Children of Men*.

The thing about me as a producer, if you look at my résumé, you cannot figure out why I made the movies that I did. Almost every movie that I actually care about is about code and choices. That was what *Spy Game* was about, code. *Family Man* was about what was the right choice, which way do you go. That's kind of a synopsis.

Each one has a story—how they almost came apart, how they almost didn't get made. I loved working on *Spy Game* with Tony Scott, who was a really good guy. What's funny about producing is that it's all pretty much about willpower.

What's been a frustration?

The thing that has been the hardest for me is that I've always wanted to be a director, and it's taken so long to get to that. I bought the rights to *Flash of Genius*. I was just absolutely determined to make that movie. Well, it took ten years. That's been my only frustration because I love directing, and I love writing. When people see a movie like that, they expect it to be corny. That movie's not corny. Greg Kinnear's performance is so demanding. That character pushes you—frustrates you, really gets you angry. He kisses off settlements. It's really a movie about principle. It's about, "What is the cost of fighting for a principle?" It comes at great cost. It may be worth it, or it may not be worth it. That is a decision that someone has to make. If you go up against superior odds for something you believe in, it's going to cost you.

I loved directing *Flash of Genius.* I guess I would have preferred directing the last 15 years instead of producing, but now I'm in a position to do that. I've had a lot of support from a lot of people.

It's been three years since the last one. There are a bunch of projects that I really love that I haven't gotten going. There's a book I've always wanted to make, *American Ambassador.* That was always one of the movies that I just felt badly that I've never gotten going.

The movies I have been involved with as a producer have been really great experiences. You get a reputation as a guy who shows up, and always delivers. Responsible. My frustrations have been that I want to direct. I want to direct ten movies, so I've got to get on it. I loved directing *Flash of Genius.*

ABRAHAM'S FILMOGRAPHY

Producer
I Saw the Light (2015)
The Man with the Iron Fists 2 (2015)
RoboCop (2014)
The Last Exorcism Part II (2013)
The Man with the Iron Fists (2012)
In Time (2011)
The Thing (2011)
The Last Exorcism (2010)
Let's Go to Prison (2006)
Children of Men (2006)
Dawn of the Dead (2004)
The Rundown (2003)
The Emperor's Club (2002)
Tuck Everlasting (2002)
Spy Game (2001)
The Family Man (2000)
Bring It On (2000)
Trippin' (1999)

Playing God (1997)
A Thousand Acres (1997)

Executive Producer
Slither (2006)
Thirteen Days (2000)
End of Days (1999)
The Hurricane (1999)
For Love of the Game (1999)
Air Force One (1997)
The Baby-Sitters Club (1995)
The Road to Wellville (1994)
Princess Caraboo (1994)
Sugar Hill (1993)
A Midnight Clear (1992)

Co-Producer
The Commitments (1991)

Director
I Saw the Light (2015)
Flash of Genius (2008)

Tony Bill

A consummate independent producer-director who started his career as an actor, Tony Bill produced The Sting *(1973), for which he shared the Academy Award for Best Picture with Michael Phillips and Julia Phillips. He is credited with discovering* The Sting's *Oscar-winning writer, David S. Ward.*

Prior to The Sting, *he produced Ward's first script,* Steelyard Blues, *a dark comedy starring Peter Boyle and Donald Sutherland, set amid the detritus of American society: auto graveyards, strip bars and porn theaters.*

Bill has produced a mix of motion pictures many featuring first-time writers and directors. His other films include Deadhead Miles, Hearts of the West, Untamed Heart, Five Corners *and* Going in Style. *All were initially optioned outside the studio system with his own money.*

Beginning with his first feature film project, Deadhead Miles, *written by newcomer Terrence Malick, Bill established a reputation for finding undiscovered talent and producing off-the-beaten-track projects. He produces and directs the kinds of films that many in the commercial industry would have considered gambles, particularly because they feature new writing, directing and acting talent.*

Bill had an eye for undiscovered talent and often collaborated with newcomers, either as a director or a producer. He actively sought non–Hollywood material from a vast array of untraditional sources: prison journals, obscure newspapers, unsolicited manuscripts. For his directorial debut My Bodyguard, *the story of a boy who enlists his new school's most intimidating student, he also found a new writer, Alan Ormsby.*

The romance thriller Five Corners, *set in a working-class neighborhood of Queens, was the first script of John Patrick Shanley, who went on to write* Moonstruck. Untamed Heart, *a romance starring*

Tony Bill with Jennifer Drecker on the set of *Flyboys* (2006). Courtesy Barnstorm Films.

Marisa Tomei and Christian Slater, was the first produced screenplay of Tom Sierchio.

Following graduation from Notre Dame as an English major, Bill began his career as an actor in the 1960s, first appearing on screen as Frank Sinatra's younger brother in 1963's Come Blow Your Horn. *He is perhaps most recognizable for his performance as a bemused ad executive in* Shampoo. *Despite praise from critics and peers for his performances, Bill was determined to become a director, not an actor. His other films include* None but the Brave, You're a Big Boy Now, Soldier in the Rain, Never a Dull Moment *and* Ice Station Zebra. *In* Pee-wee's Big Adventure *he played a movie mogul. On TV, he was hailed for his performance as Lee Harvey Oswald in a BBC dramatization.*

Bill began directing in 1978, adapting O. Henry's classic short story "The Ransom of Red Chief" for the Learning Corp. of America. His feature film directing credits include Six Weeks, *a drama starring Dudley Moore and Mary Tyler Moore;* Crazy People, *a comedy;* Untamed Heart,

17

a sentimental romance starring Marisa Tomei and Christian Slater; Flyboys, *a drama set in the aviation world; and* A Home of Our Own, *starring Kathy Bates as a single mother raising six children.*

More recently, Bill has earned a solid reputation as a television director, heading an array of cable productions. For network television, he directed several episodes of Chicago Hope *and* High Incident. *His list of telefilms includes* Love Thy Neighbor *with John Ritter and Penny Marshall;* One Christmas *with Katharine Hepburn and Henry Winkler;* Oliver Twist *with Richard Dreyfuss and Elijah Wood; and* A Chance of Snow, *with JoBeth Williams.*

Bill is a partner in Barnstorm Films with Helen Buck Bartlett. The duo produced the Showtime Original Pictures In the Time of Butterflies *starring Salma Hayek,* The Fixer *starring Jon Voight, and* Beyond the Call *with Sissy Spacek. In recent years he has directed a number of TV movies and series episodes.*

Bill has served on the Board of Governors of the Academy of Motion Picture Arts and Sciences and on its Board of Trustees. During the glasnost '80s, he served on the board of the American-Soviet Film Initiative, an organization devoted to creating bonds between the two countries. He formerly co-owned the restaurant 72 Market Street with the late Dudley Moore in Venice, California.

Congenial and modest, Bill has been a longtime speaker at film schools, ever willing to read unsolicited projects and to take a chance on new filmmakers.

Duane Byrge: What do you say when someone asks what you do as a producer?

Tony Bill: I have a very easy-to-understand point I tell to explain to them what they will do as a producer. I suggest to them that they are going to be a professional poker player.

What does a professional poker player do? Well, first of all he does everything he can to learn how to play the game. Then, he takes whatever stakes he can assemble. He borrows money, sells his house, asks his rich uncle for a loan. He saves up and does whatever it takes to get his stake.

He goes to where they play the game. He sits at the table and gets dealt hand after hand, after hand. Some he plays. Now and then he gets good cards. He bets a little, or he bets all in. But all the while he plays these hands.

What he's doing is a combination of skill and luck. He may get a hand that doesn't look good, but his skill allows him to play it well. He may get a terrific hand and not play it well. But there is no one standing over his shoulder who can tell him how he should have done it or should be doing it.

In retrospect, it is easy to tell someone how to do something. During the play it is pretty hard to say how he should be doing it. You could say how you would do it, but not how he should do it.

Whether he's a veteran player or new to the table, he's still a professional poker player, and he's going to be going from game to game. Plus, the game is going to start all over again with each new hand. So, you think of a hand as a script. What you are doing as a producer is what a poker player does with a hand. You will be reading it, but you may be so uninterested in it that you don't finish reading it. You may read it and think about it, what to do about it. You may read it and decide to pursue it. You may decide to option it. You may decide to spend a lot of money on the option or $10. You may decide to spend six months or a lifetime on it.

The script that you get is the luck of the draw. What you do with it is your skill. The only difference is that you are not playing with your friends, but that doesn't matter. You're playing against the odds, you're playing against your chances of winning, which is making a movie at all, much less a successful one.

You are a professional poker player. There's no difference. You have no job security, and each time you come to the table it's different—a new hand to be played a different way. Each script is different, each movie different. So, I don't see the difference between a producer and a professional poker player.

When you started out, you found material that other people had passed on, hadn't read, didn't pursue. Diamonds in the rough.

Well, almost every movie I have made is by a first-time writer—Terrence Malick, Paul Schrader and Rob Thompson. I am very attracted to the unknown. I am very attracted to the long shot. Maybe the gambler in me that wants to go to the horse races and bet on the 50-to-1 shot, not on the sure thing.

How did you come upon David Ward's script The Sting?

An agent sent me a script called *Steelyard Blues*, written by a young man who just came out of college. I read it, and I thought that it showed real writing talent. I thought the script would be a tough movie to get made, but I loved the quality and the originality of the writing.

I really wanted to meet this guy. We met and talked and eventually the conversation turned to, "What do you want to do next?" He said, "I have this idea about a young guy in his thirties who's a con man. His best friend gets killed and he tries to con the guy who killed him out of every dollar."

That was about it. I said I loved that idea. We didn't talk about it more than five minutes, maybe less. It was very simple, a bare-boned concept. I said, "I've got to do it." So, that's how it happened. Then I went around looking for someone to help me option or pay for it. Ultimately I met Julia and Michael Phillips. We formed a company. We got *Steelyard Blues* made. We got the rights, too, for *The Sting*, to do after that. It took David a couple years to write *The Sting*.

What made you switch gears from acting to become a producer?

Well, from the day I arrived in Hollywood, even though it was a complete new territory to me, I felt unsatisfied with two of the aspects of being a movie star. The first was that you have to wait for someone to call you to do something. The second was that I was not comfortable with being a public figure.

I was treated well, all that kind of stuff. I was a young guy out of college. I wasn't going to beach parties and surfing, doing all the things the movies said a guy of my generation was doing. The movies they were making for my age group were all silly, adolescent movies.

So, I started asking the producers and directors why there were no movies that actually addressed our lives or interests. They were very welcoming of my thoughts. They said, "What do you think? We like your ideas." They encouraged me to express my ideas.

I read a book I thought would make a good movie, a book called *The Graduate*. Then I heard somebody else had optioned it, so I thought, "Well, maybe I am not out of touch. Maybe I am on the right track."

Then I met this young guy named Terry Malick. He was at the AFI and a friend of a friend. We just connected. That's how I got my first movie made. I brought him an idea for a movie based on truck-driving music. He did the script, and that's how that was born.

Hearts of the West *was a favorite of mine when it came out.*

That's my favorite of all the movies I have produced. That movie contradicted my own inclination: I [was] not interested in making a movie about Hollywood, but I just fell in love with the script. It is not about the Hollywood of today. It's kind of a little bit of a mythological Hollywood, as well as being a very realistic Hollywood of its era.

I was sitting in a café one day and a friend of mine introduced me to a friend of his named Rob Thompson. Rob is from Seattle and was in town looking for an agent for his script. He just wrote his first script. I told him I was a producer and that I read scripts. He gave me his script. Again, I was struck by the originality and freshness. I have a kind of fatal attraction to offbeat, fresh scripts.

The problem with that is that they are very hard to sell. They are very hard to get made. Also, I don't like movies that are like other movies. In fact, I would like to think that every movie I make is unique rather than a tradition or a genre. They are not like any movie that you've seen before.

I don't get much made. I don't respond positively enough to just a good generic script, or a project that can be explained in shorthand by referring to other movies. That kind of a description is a total turn-off to me. I know that they are not thinking originally. As a result, it takes me a long time for me to read them, and I've never made one like that. I always tell writers to avoid synopses, if they can. It makes their movie or script sound stupid.

You produced and directed **Five Corners***. Did you have a conflict between being a producer and a director?*

Well, for me there's an inner conflict between producing and directing in the sense that as a director I never take off my producer's hat. I am always cost and time conscious as a director. So, even if am directing someone else's movie, where it's their problem, I don't consider it their problem. I consider it mine. I am very compulsively time-conscious. I just don't take lightly or easily the idea of being behind schedule or spending any more money than needs to be spent on something. My producer's hat is always on, and I can't take it off.

I think that my strength as a director comes from the fact that I can totally go with the flow. I can cope with anything that gets thrown at me. I can deal with any emergencies, any surprise, any deprivation, any change of plan. I am very good at just getting it done, however we have to do it. My weakness as a director is that I don't plan much, if that's a weakness. I try not to make plans.

As a producer you kind of know what's going to happen, where you shoot tomorrow. I discovered that my way of working as a director is to say to myself, "I don't know what I am going to do until I am on the set." In general, I don't make plans. I work it out when I get there with the actors.

If I were producing a movie, I am not sure I would enjoy the director telling me he is not sure what we are going to do that day. Also, I have an attitude that you can do anything for any amount of money. That is to say, you could make any movie for any price. The thing is, it wouldn't be the same as with more money. So, within certain constraints, my attitude towards budget is, you tell me how much it's worth to you and that's how much we will make it for.

It's really insane that a studio would ask a producer how much a movie would cost. What does it matter what it would cost? It will cost how much you are willing to pay for it. Now, if it's not worth $5 million to you, tell me it's only worth $3 million. If you think it's not going to be good enough at $5 million, tell me if you would be willing to spend $7 million. Why would you ask me what it's going to cost?

It's like you are forced to say how much it's going to cost—you know, put in more camels or something. That's not what it's about. What it's about is what it's worth to the studio to make this investment in this movie. Are they going to get a good movie for it? Well, if they only are only going to pay you $1 million for the movie, maybe none of us are going to like the way it's going to turn out. Or, maybe we will.

When Helen [Bartlett] and I made *Untamed Hearts* at MGM, the MGM budget was going to be $12 million.

That was a lot at that time.

Well, MGM lost their enthusiasm for the movie because we didn't have big stars in it. They said, "Can you make it with Cher or Madonna?" We said, "Well, yeah, but we don't think it's going to be the movie that was written." I asked, "Why don't you let me hire a kind of unknown actor that I want, named Brad Pitt."

They said, "Well, he's not a movie star. We don't want to make it with him."

"Well, how about we make it with somebody else?"

They said, "How about Christian Slater?" So, I went to see Christian Slater. I think Christian had never been in anything like this.

Eventually, we finally had a meeting at MGM—kind of like a "do or die" meeting. They said that they didn't want to spend $12 million and asked what we thought we could make it for. I told them that I could make it for any amount of money you give me, so why don't you tell me what it's worth to you, and that would be the budget. They said, "Could you make it for $6 million?" And I said, "Thank you very much. That's the budget, that's a deal." That's what we made it for.

You got a really great performance out of a young actress named Marisa Tomei, who didn't cost as much as Cher or Madonna.

I think very often constraints are healthier than surplus. Not having enough money has made more good movies than having all you want. If I were to make a list of really wonderful movies, you would find out that nearly all were made under financial limits, if not duress. They were turned down over and over and over by various people—directors, actors, studios. And they didn't have everything they wanted to make the movie with.

You never get your first choice, which is probably good. So, anyway, we got Christian to read the script, and he said he would do it. And then he called back a couple of days later and said he had changed his mind, he wasn't going to do it. We thought that was our only chance with MGM. They said they were willing to do it for $6 million with Christian.

I didn't have the slightest idea of how to talk to him into it, how to talk to somebody about something that they have turned down. Helen and I got into a car on a Sunday—he was directing a children's play in Beverly Hills. We went to see the play, and we went to see him afterwards. I was sure that Helen could talk him into it. She can talk anybody into anything. But, because I was directing it, I was the guy who had to do the talking. I had no idea what to say. I didn't have a plan. I just wanted to talk him into doing it.

So we cornered him backstage after the play. He couldn't get away. Suddenly, a bright light went off in my brain, probably fueled by adrenaline and fear. I said to him, "I know why you don't want to do this movie. It's because you're afraid to be on screen without a gun or without a smart remark. Everything you've done has had a bit of finger-snapping."

I said, "Every actor is afraid of being on screen with nothing to do. And this part has nothing to do. Throughout the movie, you almost don't do anything. And I promise you, I am not going to let you do anything. I am not going to let you be the smart-ass. I am not going to let you be the hip young guy. And, I am not going to let you do any of that winking and smiling with one side of your face. I am going to give you absolutely nothing. The hardest thing that an actor can do is what I am going to ask you to do."

He got it. He said, "Okay, I trust you." And, it changed his career. I am really proud of Christian. He did a great job, and that's how that movie got made.

Can you talk about some projects that got away?

Both Helen and I, we don't let them get away. I don't think so anyway. They still live in our efforts to think of a new approach. I think that people don't realize that the gestation period for a good movie is five, ten years. I think it takes at least five years to get a good movie made. It is kind of a perverse job for a grown-up.

You've said that each of the films you've produced was kind of like an experiment to see if you still wanted to continue to produce.

It's true, it's like, "Oh man, here we are, we asked for it, now we are stuck with it. What's going on here?"

It helps to have a partner who is enthusiastic. For me, it helps to appreciate that every movie that I have made is one nobody wanted to do originally. It's just not automatic. It's not, "Hey, Tony, what do you want to do next?"

I think it's the lot of the producer. Producers are not perceived to have skills. So, people don't really ask you to produce a movie. You find a script that you want to get made. And you're back to square one on each time—that's producing.

Take a guy like Jerry Hellman. He hasn't made a lot of movies but his movies are arguably the best movie his directors ever made. *Coming Home*, for instance. Or take a look at Saul Zaentz. When Saul Zaentz is the producer on a movie, you know you are in for a serious approach to making a movie.

After you have finished with post-production and your movie is done, what is the producers' job? How involved are you in the marketing and promotion?

As involved as they will let me be. I do feel strongly about the ad campaign. I do like to get involved in the ad campaign. On *My Bodyguard*, the studio came up with a last-minute ad for the movie and I just thought it was terrible. Basically I said, "I can do better than that." The ad they had reminded me of a cover of a comic book. It was a comic book approach to the movie. And this was the eleventh hour. It was actually already in some of the theaters. Their ad totally pissed me off. I said, "Why not take an image from the movie—two kids on the motorcycle with their hands up in the air—and use it in the ad as a single image?"

Hearts of the West, by the way, is a good example of the ads that I approved and probably shouldn't have. The movie had great reviews and opened at the New York Film festival. The next day it opened theatrically, and nobody went.

I think one of the mistakes on that movie as a producer—I take full blame for it—was that I think the title was misleading. It made people think it was a Western. The ad art reinforced that misconception, made it look like it was a Western. Nobody wanted to go see an old Western. I think the title and the ad art were misleadingly good. They were right but they were wrong.

People are always confused in the movie business about what you do and why you do it. Producing is a very time-consuming thing. As I said, my wife is a producer. She produced *North Country* a couple of years go. We like to produce together, but it's hard for us to do things at the same time. Sometimes she produces something I don't direct. Sometimes I direct something that she doesn't produce. I have my favorite things. She has her favorite things. In general, I have produced much less since I started directing.

What is the function of a producer once the movie is filming? Do you get involved with the dynamics, the personal things that arise?

Exactly. That's the producers' job—to make people get along. Focus on the creative point of view and the personal point of view like, "Hey, be nice, be quiet, be kind, be gentle and be civilized." It's kind of like being a referee sometimes. A referee between the studio and the director, the director and the actor. As the producer, you become the referee and it's not the most fun part of the job. But I think it is a good job for the producer to enforce the creative collaboration between people.

You have a congenial personality. Obviously, you can be forceful in that way.

Well, I like to think that I have a pretty logical mind. I can make my points strongly, without yelling or screaming or pulling, or going behind people's back. I like to think that I make sense, when it's necessary. I don't need to win the argument just because I am the producer. I am not interested in winning the argument for its own sake but for the movie's sake.

Again, that's for better or worse, because there are people that do well by being forceful and very confrontational. But it's not me.

BILL'S FILMOGRAPHY

Producer
Untamed Heart (1993)
Five Corners (1987)
Going in Style (1979)
The Little Dragons (1979)
Hearts of the West (1975)
The Sting (1973)
Steelyard Blues (1973)
Deadhead Miles (1972)

Executive Producer
The Little Dragons (1979)
Boulevard Nights (1979)

Harry and Walter Go to New York (1976)

Director
Flyboys (2006)
A Home of Our Own (1993)
Untamed Heart (1993)
Crazy People (1990)
Five Corners (1987)
Six Weeks (1982)
My Bodyguard (1980)

Bona Fide Productions: Albert Berger and Ron Yerxa

Albert Berger and Ron Yerxa have produced some of the more off-beat, satirical looks at mainstream culture in the last two decades. Their breakout project was the comedy Election, *directed by Alexander Payne. Their company, Bona Fide Productions, has become well regarded for its intelligent independent films. They received a Best Picture Oscar nomination for* Nebraska, *also directed by Payne.*

*The duo has worked with a range of top directors, including Steven Soderbergh (*King of the Hill*), Anthony Minghella (*Cold Mountain*), Todd Field (*Little Children*) and Jonathan Dayton and Valerie Faris (*Little Miss Sunshine, Ruby Sparks*).*

*Berger and Yerxa work outside the studio gates, yet flourish with a mix of studio support and independent spirit. They have strong relationships with mainstream companies such as Fox Searchlight and Paramount. They are also collaborative and pragmatic, having partnered on several films with other production companies, including Mirage (*Cold Mountain*) and Wildwood (*King of the Hill*).*

Their prowess emanates from the duo's low-key congeniality, allowing them to maintain and nurture a wide spectrum of relationships.

More recent films produced under their Bona Fide banner include Ruby Sparks, The Necessary Death of Charlie Countryman, Nebraska, Low Down *and* Louder Than Bombs.

Berger and Yerxa received "Producer of the Year" honors from the PGA. They have won two independent Spirits Awards for Best Feature: Election *(1999) and* Little Miss Sunshine *(2006).*

In addition, Cold Mountain *and* Little Miss Sunshine *were nominated by BAFTA as Best Film, while* Cold Mountain *was also nominated for the Alexander Korda Award for Best British Film.*

Berger and Yerxa joined forces for the first time as Bona Fide when they produced Steven Soderbergh's King of the Hill. *At the 1989 Sundance Film Festival the duo wandered into the first screening of Soderbergh's* Sex, Lies and Videotape. *After the film, they invited the director to have coffee and asked him to consider turning Tobias Wolff's novel* This Boy's Life *into a film. Soderbergh read and respected the book, but suggested exploring A.E. Hotchner's memoir* King of the Hill *instead, a book he had long admired.*

Soderbergh, however, was already committed to making the film Kafka. *In the interim, Berger and Yerxa took day jobs: Berger at Marvin Worth Productions and Yerxa at Sovereign Pictures. They officially founded Bona Fide in 1992, with the start of production of* King of the Hill.

The duo has a feel for spotting books that are not obvious choices. They struck gold in Tom Perrotta's desk drawer, with his unpublished novel Election. *Since then, they have explored adapting several of Perrotta's books into films, resulting in* Little Children *(New Line) and* The Leftovers *(HBO). They have produced several other projects from books, including Charles Frazier's* Cold Mountain, *Scott Phillips'* Ice Harvest, *Myla Goldberg's* Bee Season *and A.J. Albany's* Low Down.

They are also game to explore original projects with new talent. Little Miss Sunshine *was a screenplay by first-time writer Michael Arndt and first-time, husband-and-wife directing team Jonathan Dayton and Valerie Faris.*

Little Miss Sunshine *became a huge critical and commercial success. Due to the Academy rule, which limited "Produced By" credits to three producers, they were not officially Oscar-nominated. Since they had found and developed the script and were accredited by the PGA, it was a controversial situation and it led to a change in the Academy's rules the following year.*

Outside of their partnership at Bona Fide, Berger executive-produced the documentary Crumb *and Yerxa executive-produced* Jack the Bear *for 20th Century–Fox.*

Albert Berger is a native of Chicago and a graduate of Tufts University. After college, he returned to Chicago where he owned and managed the Sandburg Theatre, a revival house that showcased classic and obscure films. He attended film school at Columbia University and then

moved to Los Angeles and wrote scripts for a number of studios. He
served as Vice-President of development for Marvin Worth Productions.

After Ron Yerxa graduated from Stanford University, he taught in
the "Upward Bound" program and then received a graduate degree from
the University of California–Santa Cruz. He moved to Los Angeles and
opened a storefront school site before beginning his film career at CBS
Films and at Sovereign Films. He then became an independent producer.

ALBERT BERGER

*Duane Byrge: You started out with movies in your native Chi-
cago.*

Albert Berger: After college I owned and ran the Sandburg Movie
Theater on Dearborn and Division. It was a repertory theater. We
would show double features, which changed three times a week, sort

of like the American Cinema-
teque, CineFamily or the New
Beverly. We had some first-run
films, German New Wave films.
We showed *Peeping Tom*, and
older stuff, Hitchcock stuff. It was
an interesting place. There were a
lot of patrons who went on to
prominence: Richard Pena, who
runs the New York Film Festival,
wrote program notes there. Mark
Romanek was an usher. Ken
Kwapis used to show up. It was a
stimulating environment. There's
a Walgreens there now.

*When did you become
interested in film?*
I caught the bug in high
school. I was an English, poli-sci
major in college, but I also studied

**Albert Berger, 2013. Courtesy Bona
Fide Productions.**

29

film, and did this movie theater for a year and a half. After we went out of business, I headed to Columbia Film School in New York. I studied screenwriting-directing there. At the time, Milos Forman and Frank Daniel were in charge of the program. Frank was my mentor.

I was a screenwriter for the first ten years that I was in Los Angeles and my partner was Dave Weber, a friend from Columbia. We did a lot of stuff for Garry Marshall. I primarily wrote comedies. We sold a couple scripts to TriStar. We went on to write for Paramount and MGM. The thing about it was, they were movies that I gained employment writing, but they weren't the movies that I was on fire to see made.

The scripts that I felt strongly about were the ones we wrote on spec and weren't able to sell. At a certain point, it somehow dawned on me that becoming a producer was a much clearer path to being able to make movies that I cared about in a deep way. As a producer you can sort of write your own ticket, do it your own way. That was a big revelation. There was the equal realization that writing was not all that close to filmmaking. In fact, you were divorced from the process. On the other hand, as a producer you are the first one in and the last one out. That was something that never occurred to me in film school.

I had no interest in producing when I was at Columbia. Everybody wanted to be a director. It was a profound realization that as a producer you could shape your own projects, and also work on many different things at the same time. Sometimes you might be developing a script while other projects might be in post. The variety you find at any given time keeps your engagement up.

It struck me that as a director you can be stuck working on a project exclusively for three years or more. As a producer you get the advantage of all sides of it. It never occurred to me in ten years as a writer that producing would be a gratifying way to be involved with films that you care about.

You've got that business gene part of you too.

Probably to some degree, but I really think it's the same impulse that drew me to writing and directing that also brought me to producing. We're very much creative producers. I come from more of a writing orientation than Ron. Having sat on the other side of the fence and being given notes and trying to figure out what the studio wants and how to get from A to B, and having studied and written screenplays, it all makes me feel empathetic with the writers.

Ron is more connected out in the world. He has been at it longer. Ron has a lot of relationships in the town, but I wouldn't say that either of us are particularly business-oriented. There's a kind of personal aspect to our movies. The money side of it is always more complicated. These are tricky, interesting films that sometimes do great and sometimes don't. But we completely stand by them creatively. It's always a struggle to try to put them together because the numbers aspect of it is not really our strong suit. But somehow we manage to figure out how to get them made. They get made, and I really love the movies we've done. But you can't really point to our slate and say that these movies make business sense in the way that Jerry Bruckheimer's make sense.

Can you talk about your early days as partners?

We started at Sundance in 1989, when we got thrown out of a party, went across the street and saw the very first screening of *Sex, Lies & Videotape*. At the time we were trying to get *This Boy's Life* made. We went up to Steven Soderbergh after the screening and started talking about *This Boy's Life*. The conversation turned to *King of the Hill*, which was a book that he wanted to adapt that was similar. As Soderbergh's star rose, we were able to set up *King of the Hill* at Universal. This was our first opportunity to make a film with a strong independent filmmaker within a studio context. It was an approach we were very comfortable with and we tried to repeat it as often as possible.

You can't really say that we make independent films in the way that Christine Vachon or Ted Hope do, and you can't really say that we make films within the studio model, like say Scott Rudin or Art Linson—the kind of bigger, studio-quality movies. We're somewhere in between, balancing the independent world and studio.

You're in the seams there, doing your own thing, but you're able to work in both worlds.

It started in the beginning with Soderbergh. Then we repeated the approach with Alexander Payne. He made *Citizen Ruth* independently. We brought him *Election* and made it at Paramount. We did the same thing with Todd Field, Dayton and Faris, and Siegel and McGehee. We are consistently trying to navigate the world between studios and indies.

King of the Hill—*didn't you ally with Wildwood on that?*

Yes, Robert Redford through his relationship with Paul Newman had access to A.E. Hotchner, who wrote the novel. Steven wanted Redford's help in convincing Hotchner to let him write that adaptation. We were friendly with Barbara Malty, who was running Wildwood at the time. She lined us up with Redford as executive producer and he helped get the rights to the book.

***You ally with somebody powerful, like on* Cold Mountain.**

I think that the earlier part of our career was all about aligning with more significant production companies in order to get things done. *Cold Mountain* was with Mirage. That was a huge undertaking and we needed a strong production entity as an umbrella, both to land the project and make the movie.

They would legitimize you guys, so to speak.

Exactly. It also meant that we were sharing the load with somebody like Sydney Pollack, who had great experience and knew everything there was to know about producing. We got a lot out of those partnerships. Now we're doing more and more on our own.

Can you talk about Bona Fide's beginning?

Our first movie, *King of the Hill*, was made in 1992. But we set up the project in 1989. So we had to wait for Soderbergh to make *Kafka*. He said he would make *King of the Hill* next and we were all worried that he would find something else to do and ditch the project. But he stayed true to his word.

It's funny how that's worked out for us: Filmmakers keeping their word on small projects while continuously being offered bigger ones. It worked that way with Alexander Payne on *Nebraska*. Ron had the idea that we would go to Alexander, and maybe he would mentor a young emerging filmmaker. We'd produce it, and Alexander would exec-produce it. He said, "Well, I actually have an idea who should direct it. It should be me." But he didn't want to do three road-trip movies in a row. He had just done *About Schmidt,* and he was about to do *Sideways.* He said if we wait for him till his next film, he would do it afterwards. It took Alexander six years to make *The Descendants.* But he remained true to his word and jumped right into *Nebraska* afterwards.

Tell us about Cold Mountain.

That project was kind of a remarkable, fortuitous thing. I was browsing at Book Soup and picked up the book after it had been passed on in manuscript by everybody, but before it had been reviewed. I had a personal interest in that part of the country, the Blue Ridge Mountains and the Appalachians. So I read it, and was blown away.

Coincidentally, Ron and I had business with an agent, Lynn Pleshette, on another project, and she also represented *Cold Mountain.* We asked her if we could shop it around. She must have thought, "What's to lose? These guys are interested and they're credible"—we were about to start *Election.* So Lynn let us run around with it.

Within the first two weeks of shopping *Cold Mountain,* a couple of things happened. First, we went to Sydney Pollack through an old friend Bill Horberg who worked and produced at Mirage. Sydney was busy acting in *Eyes Wide Shut* but Bill had the idea to go to [Anthony] Minghella. Meanwhile the book got reviewed to insane acclaim. All of a sudden, we had our hands on this very hot property and we had the boost of those reviews. Then, of course, competition came because of the very same reviews. Although Lynn was allowing us to shop it, she was not going to turn down a major offer from a competitor.

Basically, we lined up our team. We were producing with Mirage and Minghella was going to write and direct. Then it came down to convincing Charles Frazier that we were the right option. Also, we needed to figure out who was going to buy the project.

At the time, we had also submitted it to MGM/UA. Lindsay Doran was running the place and she had been formerly head of production at Mirage. So that became our strongest option. MGM/UA ended up putting up the money for the book. It took many years to develop the project. There were several drafts of the script, and it was a whole very elaborate dynamic. By then, Miramax had bought the project from

MGM and Harvey [Weinstein] had a long-standing relationship with both Mirage and with Anthony and he badly wanted to make the film. It became a question of casting and budget and how that all fit together to unlock a green light.

It was a very difficult time for us because our desire to produce that book in the first place had everything to do with the specific region of the country, North Carolina and the Blue Ridge Mountains, that the book took place in. But it became apparent that the only way to make that movie was to go to Romania.

We scouted North Carolina extensively. We budgeted there and it was going to cost well over $100 million. Harvey just wasn't going to finance it for that number. We were able to save a good 20, 30 million by filming it in Romania. We scouted all over the place in North Carolina, and the area we had pinpointed for filming was Transylvania County. Later, when we ended up settling on Romania, the Transylvania Mountains became our primary location. We realized that early settlers of the North Carolina mountains region must have had made the connection because of the similar landscape. The savings in Romania also allowed our production designer to create an entire town from scratch for an affordable amount.

It just became a numbers thing. We were demoralized because it was our very strong intention to make the film in North Carolina. By then, we had a good relationship with Charles Frazier and we knew how much it meant to him. We almost got thrown off the movie because of our advocacy for North Carolina. But eventually Harvey forgave us and we were able to stay on.

We ended up having a great experience. It was absolutely the best crew that you could ever imagine. People like costume designer Ann Roth, who I think is the most impressive person I've met in film business, or John Seale and Dante Ferretti and Walter Murch. Anthony was about the most generous-spirited guy you would ever want to meet and he presided over the movie with the best blend of being a consummate artist and great collaborator. I worked closely with T-Bone. I went down to Nashville for the particularly exciting bluegrass pre-records, and many musicians that I admired were working with T-Bone Burnett. Music was an area that I really got to step into.

Ron and I figured out a working relationship with Sydney, Anthony and Bill Horberg. Bill is an old friend of mine and we ran that theater back in Chicago together. Bill was our point-of-entry into Mirage. Each of us had our area. Ron, Bill and I were all producers and Sydney was over all of us. He was the pre-eminent director-producer of his time, the gold standard. You had to know when to take the back seat to Sydney. At certain crucial moments he stepped forward to lead the way. For me, I don't think I'll ever be around a group like that again. It was really the "A Team."

The movie may not have come out perfectly. Personally, I think there was a longer cut of *Cold Mountain* that was the best version. Fifteen or twenty minutes got taken out late in the process and the movie suffered. It's hard to argue that a two-and-a-half-hour movie is too short but I think that was the case with *Cold Mountain*. More would have been better. Also, you have to wonder how much we lost by not filming in North Carolina. Did the film lose a little of the book's special quality with a European approach? We'll never know. But given the choice of making the movie or not, I say "Make the movie."

One point to make is that producing involves elaborate collaborations. Like *Cold Mountain*, *Little Miss Sunshine* was a prime example. Michael Arndt sent us his screenplay. We knew Michael because he had been Matthew Broderick's assistant on *Election*. We loved the script and brought it to financier Marc Turtletaub, who was just starting out as a producer and had formed a company with David Friendly. We had a first-look deal with them and we all partnered up on *Little Miss Sunshine*. Ron and I also brought Jonathan Dayton and Valerie Faris to the project. Marc and David agreed they were the right choice to direct.

Shortly after joining forces, we set up the project at Focus. We spent three years trying to get it going but to no avail. Finally Marc decided to finance the film on his own and we were able to get it back from Focus. The script had been rewritten but we had been able to reinstate Michael's original draft. At this point Marc had parted ways with David Friendly and now had a company with Peter Saraf. So from this point on there were five producers on *Little Miss Sunshine*.

Everything in its time.
We were the ones who found the script for *Little Miss Sunshine*, and we were the ones who were on it from beginning to end. Marc

Turtletaub was completely involved with all aspects of the film and financed the movie. David Friendly had been involved from the time we gave it to Marc and had a hand in critical casting moves. Peter Saraf was on the set every day and guided the film from prep through post. The thing for me is that you find your place. The goal is to make a movie, and not to sit on set for 15 of 24 days. The goal is to figure out the best way to collaborate with other people in order to make the best movie possible.

These days we're mostly producing on our own. But we remain open to partnerships and always look for the best ways to work together to benefit a film. Each film has its own flow, its own set of partnerships and its own dynamic. Each film is rewarding in different ways.

That's been our evolution. From books that slipped through the cracks to screenplays. Always operating in that area between the studios and independents.

There is something exciting about finding and getting involved with a director who has made a successful film in the independent realm, and figuring out how to work it on a bigger scale.

Lately, I'm finding that the harder films are the most interesting. They don't necessarily make the best movies. But there is something exciting about when you're in a wildly improvisational mode as opposed to where you always know where the movie is going. We just experienced the two kinds of extremes back to back. *Charlie Countryman* was an anything-goes experience with director Fredrik Bond using the unique unpredictable character of Bucharest as well as the distinct temperaments of cast members to enhance the movie. *Nebraska* was very much Alexander Payne's vision. It was fascinating to watch him execute that. The experiences couldn't have been more different.

In our early days as producers, the only material we were able to get our hands on were books that had slipped through the cracks. Either they had been passed on by other people because they weren't obvious movies or we stumbled on to them just before they were discovered by the critics. Books to movies became our thing. *Bee Season, Ice Harvest, Cold Mountain, King of the Hill.*

Election was an unpublished manuscript. The publishing world didn't know whether it was young-adult fiction or literary fiction. Weirdly, the book got published as a result of the movie. At the time,

36

Tom Perrotta he had only written *Bad Haircut*, which was a collection of short stories. *Election* was an unpublished manuscript at the time we first read it.

How do you find an unpublished novel?

It was through a friend of ours who was at a writers' colony with Tom. She called and said, "There's a great fiction writer who is working on a novel called *The Wishbones*." She thought there was a strong movie in *The Wishbones* and she suggested we approach him. We read *Bad Haircut* and loved it.

We called Tom up. We said, "We've heard about *The Wishbones*, and we'd like to read it." He said it wasn't finished yet, but he had this unpublished novel, *Election*, that he couldn't figure out what to do with. He described it, and it sounded great. It sounded like our kind of movie. We read it, and we brought it to David Gale who was running MTV Films. They got excited as well. *Election* was set in a high school. They felt it could have a great soundtrack and really give a fresh perspective on the student-teacher dynamic.

I immediately thought that Alexander Payne could be an excellent director for this. He was in post-production on *Citizen Ruth*, which I had an opportunity to see a rough cut of. I thought this guy was perfect for *Election*, and then it became a process of convincing MTV and Paramount to hire him. It took until *Citizen Ruth* screened at Sundance to great acclaim for everyone to jump on board.

Sundance opened all the doors. So, MTV and Paramount agreed to hire Alexander and Jim to write the screenplay. From the very beginning there was an interesting misunderstanding of what this movie was. Alexander was equally drawn to the adult story of a frustrated teacher trying to have an affair with his best friend's wife as he was to the stories of the younger characters. MTV and Paramount had in mind something for the teenage demographic. As producers you hope to push any misunderstandings towards the end of the process so you can make your movie before the jig is up.

They wanted something more John Hughes–ish?

Exactly. And they wanted stars in the leading role. You know it started with "You have to find Tom Hanks or Tom Cruise to play the lead." Somehow through the negotiation of all that, we ended up with Matthew Broderick, who was perfect. It became a very uncharacteristic film for MTV/Paramount to make.

The wonderful thing about MTV, it wasn't what they expected, but they completely embraced it. They just thought, "Okay, maybe this isn't going to work for kids, but we love this. We're proud to be involved with it." They were our perfect ally. It couldn't have been a better collaboration.

The Wood—*was that MTV?*

That was. David Gale, who was our great partner over there, was responsible for that. *The Wood* came through the Sundance labs. Ron has had a very long, tight relationship with Michelle Satter and the lab. We read it and really responded to it. We felt this would be good for MTV Films as a follow-up to *Election*. It's a very sweet film, and one that did very well financially. It was a wonderful, small, personal story. It was a little bit out of the main thrust of what we do. But we really liked Rick Famuyiwa and we were happy with the way it turned out.

Election is sort of the prototype of what we do. *Little Miss Sunshine* and *Ruby Sparks* as well: They all fall in as comedies with a strong social critique. Then there are projects like *Bee Season* and *King of the Hill* that are not in that mode. But they are all stories that for one reason or another we were interested in and with filmmakers that we were interested in working with. We're open to anything that grabs us in a personal way.

You jump out of your comfort zone every now and then and it works. You would be bored with one project for three years.

I would say that is an aspect of producing that we really like. Obviously, directing is an amazing thing to do. I don't put it down, but there are certain things you can do as a producer, you have the ability to work on a wide range of things that you can't do as a director.

Do you get typecast by the industry in any way? Like: "They can't do that because they did Little Miss Sunshine, *and that's not what we're looking for here"?*

Maybe people think of us as being interested exclusively in smaller films and that's just not the case. We have a desire to do studio movies on a bigger scale. Movies like *Bridesmaids*, or older movies like *Tootsie* or *Groundhog Day*. Big comedies with ideas. That's an arena that we really want to explore. Now the lines have been blurred with movies like *Silver Linings Playbook*. There are these very independent-minded movies that are made with $20 million budgets. That's got great appeal for us. And we're very enamored with what Judd Apatow is doing. We've spent a lot of time in the specialty division world. We're ready for some more studio fare.

I think you learn very different things. There is a lot to learn from Alexander Payne, and there is a lot to learn from *Countryman. The Switch* was another one—there was a lot of improvisation going on, both in our approach to making that movie as well as in literally when we were filming.

Ice Harvest?

That was an example of trying to blend very gritty noir material with a comedy director. It was sort of taking Tarantino-style material to a director from a very different world.

You guys must be voracious readers.

In the early days I read a ton of books. These days we are always trying to find scripts so we can avoid those endless years of development.

We're going through very challenging times as far as what the industry is making. Of course, it all has an effect on what we do. We make difficult films. We've stuck it out, and we're maybe having one of our most productive years with *Charlie Countryman, Nebraska* and *Low Down*. It's hard to make these smaller movies, but we're still getting them done. These are movies we really would want to see as audience members so we feel connected to them in ways that help us push forward year after year.

How about marketing? Are you involved?

We're involved with all of them. A lot went into the *Little Miss Sunshine* campaign, and the final selection of yellow as the primary color in the poster. There was a lot of conversation on all aspects of that campaign. It's a great image of everybody trying to get onto the van, which is something that, of course, we noticed people responded to every time we screened the movie. That was the moment that grabbed people. So it made sense to build the campaign around that image.

Sometimes our contribution to marketing is as simple as supporting our director's instincts. Jon and Val made great contribution to the *Little Miss Sunshine* campaign. Todd Field's ingenious trailer for *Little Children* was one of the best trailers I've ever seen. The one-sheet was also Todd's conception and it really captured the essence of the film and it was something that we really embraced. There's no point in trying to improve something that's excellent to begin with.

I feel our primary job is to get the movie done in the right way. You just hope that the movie breaks through. It becomes harder and harder to produce the kind of movies we make if they can't find an audience.

The thing that we're really trying to figure out is how to do projects on a bigger scale, in a more accessible way and to retain our sensibility. We're very happy with our independent films. Now we want to figure out how to do what we do in a big studio context.

RON YERXA

Duane Byrge: You came to movies in a roundabout way.

Ron Yerxa: Basically, I went to college and opened a street school when I moved to L.A. I became a hanger-on at the AFI, but I was never an official fellow there. It was a great creative environment and a rich oasis of film culture. And by the way, very good for contacts. I eventually met a producer there who referred me to Time-Life where I briefly wrote mini-series proposals and did some coverage.

After that brief introduction to the working film world, I got a job at CBS Theatrical Films and stayed through four different administrations. That was way back in the prehistory of '79. I was still in the wake of the counter-culture and had never had an indoor job. In 1985, I briefly joined Edgar Scherick's company and later became a production executive at Sovereign.

When Soderbergh told us he was going to make *King of the Hill*, he also said that he would have to make *Kafka* first. We wondered if there was a chance that would actually happen, but Soderbergh said, "I give you my word, I'm going to make it." So Albert and I each took a paying job, waiting for that to happen. And Soderbergh was as good as his word.

This was the gestation period when you guys realized you were going to become producers.

Unlike a lot of people, I didn't have an early interest in film. I didn't anticipate working in film. I never took a film class. Instead, my path was to just go to college [Stanford] in the mid–'60s when the counter-culture was just breaking. It was the time of Ken Kesey and the anti–Vietnam War movement. Very few students were interested in film at that time. Maybe a few had a vague interest in documentary. The whole value system was different then. Saying you want to work in film would maybe be comparable to now saying you want to go to Las Vegas to produce floor shows.

So I was hanging around Berkeley, Santa Cruz, San Francisco, and I myself became interested in documentary films. I worked briefly at a CBS affiliate as the lowest-level guy in the news doc-umentary department. I was also involved in a political group against the Vietnam War. When the war wound down, a lot of peo-ple went for university jobs and few entered the film world. One person I met was the writer Nancy Dowd [*Slap Shot*]. She had just graduated from UCLA film school and, my god, it seemed so simple back then: She wrote three scripts and had three movies going.

So I moved to Los Angeles and taught at a storefront school

Ron Yerxa, c. 2014. Courtesy Bona Fide Productions.

as a means of maintaining a subsistence living. I started hanging out at the AFI when they were at Greystone Mansion in Beverly Hills. They had a short summer program for college instructors. I was never officially a fellow, but in those days it was easy to just be there. I am grateful to AFI because it was the sort of place where you could sometimes sleep there overnight. They had superb seminars and an excellent series of films shown in a very small screening room.

I met a lot of people just by going there, hanging out and being kind of an autonomous man alone. I met a producer at AFI who asked me if I had ever considered being an executive. That was Rick Rosenberg. I hadn't really thought of it, but he generously called some people and gave me an introduction. And from that I got a job at Time-Life Films, which led to my first real job at CBS.

When did you and Albert first team up?

Albert and I decided to work together right before we went to the Sundance Film Festival in January 1989. We had met on New Year's Day 1982. A woman whom I was dating was visiting her parents who lived in Chicago. I went to see her and met Albert, who was one of her friends from high school. At that time, Albert was a graduate student at Columbia University Film School, and I was working at CBS theatrical films. But it wasn't until seven years later that we finally decided to explore being producing partners.

So in January 1989, we had casual, verbal permission to try to do something with the book *This Boy's Life*. We hadn't officially optioned it, but the agent said we could give it a run. So our goal when we met Soderbergh at the festival was to give him that book, which we did. He read it quickly, but it actually made him think of a book on the same theme that he liked from junior high, *King of the Hill.* So, ultimately he committed to work with us, but on *King of the Hill.*

We searched out a copy of *King of the Hill*, which was out of print. We found it at the UCLA Library. And for a lot of good reasons, we decided to team up with Robert Redford's company, Wildwood, which was run by a friend, Barbara Maltby. In just a few months, we had *King of the Hill* set up at Universal with Redford's company involved. But Soderbergh was going to do *Kafka* first. Albert and I were each offered a job around June after Sundance '89. I took a position with Sovereign

Pictures, and Albert took a job at Paramount with producer Marvin Worth.

Why do you feel that you didn't want to be an executive?

There are benefits and drawbacks to being a producer. One of the benefits is that you're kind of making your own world. It's often frustrating, but you are a free agent and possibly free spirit doing what you want to do. To a degree, even when you're in business as a producer with a film financed by a large corporation, you still feel like you have some personal autonomy—doing what you want to do.

As an executive, you need to be more reactive. Obviously there are a lot of benefits to being within a corporate womb. But just from a personality and psychological point of view, I never felt that being in the corporate world was a good fit for me. I bet Albert feels the same way. That idea that you have a guy over you that's ultimately second-guessing your work wasn't for me. So for all its comforts, I don't think that world was comfortable for either one of us.

Nowadays people entering the film world know so much more about the business and the whole economic context of filmmaking than we ever did. The atmosphere and expectations are radically different now. When we started, the work was so much more story- and content-oriented and so much less about the bottom line of financial models, distribution, marketing and the demographics of the audience.

Those important aspects of filmmaking weren't largely discussed in polite conversation or even industry lunches. Now people entering the business understand a lot about all those topics as they come out of film schools, or the Peter Stark Program at USC, or whatever.

You have to be optimistic. You have to be a lawyer, diplomat—wear all these different hats.

That's true. There are all those components and they're not necessarily associated skills. It's kind of like you have to drive a car, wrangle a horse, and know how to swim. They might all be necessary to do the job, but it's hard to do all these things equally well. In the past, a lot of producers probably saw themselves as content and talent nurturers and left the concrete specifics of the business to others.

What makes the producing job interesting is that you are a bit of a businessman, sometimes a creative artist, an entrepreneurial start-up person, a dab of an ethics lawyer, and often a group counselor, just trying to make things happen with the right chemistry of people.

Ultimately, as a producer you're the decider of your own destiny. If you decide to make a slasher movie, it's because you wanted to do it. It's not a mandate coming from above.

As the project progresses, eventually the writer, director and actors come to think of the project as their film. And that's a healthy way that one's ego works. But then at some point they might say, "I'm going to do it this way," and you as the producer are in the position of making things dovetail and being the constructive peacemaker.

It has to be tough if you are caught between things, either the financial and creative parts, or the studio or your creative people.

Yes, the friction could be between the director and an actor. When an actor says, "I don't see it that way, and I'm not going to play it that way." And your director says, "Well, I see it the other way," someone has to build the bridge.

You've got to somehow be a therapist and a general people-person. You have to try to talk things out, so that everyone can work together. It's a nutty thing making a film. It's like you are designing and building a car, but you are only going to make *one* of them. And once it's done, there's no improving it. Every time a film is finished, in hindsight you always feel like "God, why didn't I anticipate we didn't need that scene, or that location, or that sequence?" You have all those thoughts, but it's too late now.

You and Albert, do you have complementary skills where one of you will handle certain things and the other will do his part on something else?

We operate in a version of benign anarchy. It's not like one of us is the physical logistical guy and the other is the creative guy. We both do all of the same things. I know there are some producing partners who say, "We can finish each other's sentences." But actually we're not like that at all. We often only finish each other's sentences to contradict what the other said. We like to discuss and argue things out and bring different points of view. But we don't have a predetermined division of labor. Each time we tackle a project, we do it differently. I guess our goal is to try to match which one of us would be more productive doing a certain job.

An MBA management consultant would go crazy trying to comprehend you guys.

Yeah, if they tried to make a flow chart it would make no sense. There's not a model or a set organizational structure for us. Whatever comes up, we just try to work it out in a productive way.

This has been kind of a busy year for us because we had *Ruby Sparks* come out this past summer, and we had *Charlie Countryman* at Sundance and Berlin this year. *Nebraska* played incredibly well at Cannes this May. And we're in post-production on an independent film titled *Low Down.* Also in post is the pilot for an HBO series, *The Leftovers.* So the films are in different stages, but we're ready to ask, "What's next?" We don't have an organized pipeline, and now it's time to find something new.

You and Albert have made movies out of a lot of books. Are you inveterate readers? Do agents come to you and say, "This looks like the sort of satire Bona Fide might make"?

We get projects in a variety of ways, and about half of them come from books. I don't think it is because we're scholarly librarian types. Albert does like to go to book stores and dig around. It's not a bad place to start, obviously. But an original screenplay is the home run. Although it can be fruitful, books are a lot of work on the journey to becoming a shootable screenplay.

Tell me about some of the challenges you've faced.

We've been pretty lucky avoiding disastrous production or development episodes. *Charlie Countryman* took a long time getting off the ground. It seemed like it was going to be a $20 million film, then a 15 and then a 10. It started out as a very witty offbeat script, an inspired mash-up of genres. We really liked that about it. We developed it with a very witty writer named Matt Drake, and at various times Shia LaBeouf wanted to do it. By the time we actually got all the planets lined up to make it, the foreign market had gone down tremendously and the sales estimates were much, much lower even with such a marketable actor.

On that project, we just got into that mushy area where we would try to fine-tune the script but there was also a tug-of-war whether it needed to be an R or if it could be a PG-13. In the middle of all that turmoil, we changed directors twice. We had to ask ourselves, "Is this worth it for the ordeal?" Then out of the blue it came together again when Shia expressed a desire to do it and a new company was there to finance it at a much more modest level.

I guess an essential attribute for a producer is being flexible in your thinking—and everything else, for that matter. For example, *Charlie Countryman* was written to take place in Budapest. I took a trip there and fell in love with the city. And we seemed all set to shoot the film there. There's even a joke in the screenplay that he was supposed to go to Bucharest but ended up in Budapest. But for a lot of reasons, including financial, we reversed directions and ironically explored shooting in Bucharest, where it was cheaper to make the film.

At first that was a big disappointment, but the change actually worked better for the story, because in the revisions the main character was told by his mother to go to Bucharest which is harsh, but everyone thought "she must've meant Budapest," which is prettier. And shooting in Bucharest turned out to be great. We had a fantastic crew and loved the city.

Now in the movie, Charlie's mother comes to him in a vision and says, "I'm sorry, Charlie, I actually meant Budapest." So it worked better thematically and Bucharest was a much more interesting visual backdrop for the story with its mixture of grittiness and beauty. So although I had fought for Budapest, I was being inflexible and wrong. We ended up being much better off in Bucharest, although Budapest is the more beautiful city for other stories.

Cold Mountain *was your introduction into filming in Bucharest.*
That was a really big novel with a huge canvas. That's an open question whether the movie needed to be that big and expansive. We had to fight to secure the rights to the novel. When we first read it, it hadn't become a best seller or entered the public discussion. To make our appeal more credible, a key factor was having Anthony Minghella read the book over a weekend and he declared that he wanted to do it.

That gave our team credibility, and ultimately United Artists made a big successful offer for the rights to the book. Minghella was a partner at the production company Mirage, so we teamed up with Sydney Pollack and Bill Horberg, who were also at Mirage.

We can't say enough good things about Anthony Minghella. He was one of the greatest men we've met. Writing the screenplay was a solitary experience for him in England, but he was very receptive to comments and revisions on the script. During the production, he liked to talk to everybody on the crew—he was incredibly democratic that way. Part of his vision was to make the story beautiful in some ways, because the overall subject was so harsh.

It was a tough shoot because it was largely filmed in the winter in Romania. The big battle scenes were filmed outside of Bucharest. It happened that that was the year of the tremendous floods in Eastern Europe. So the weather and conditions were terrible and the schedule got backed up. While those battle scenes were being shot and delayed, I was in Charleston with production designer Dante Feretti and his crew waiting for the entire company to come over from Bucharest. The delays were so long that Dante and I had so many lunches and dinners together that we exhausted every possible subject of common interest.

After the battle scenes, the film came to Charleston and Virginia to shoot a variety of the scenes involving Southern life. And then the whole company moved back again to Romania, where we filmed in the mountains in the winter.

You've got to have resilience, like a dog with a bone. You face "nos" all the time.

That's a very interesting topic. In the old days you'd go to these seminars and they'd preach the passion and persistence. As if you've got to say, "I believe in this project and it's absolutely going to happen and I don't care if I get a thousand nos." But I think now people have sobered up and realized they have to ask the question: "I might be passionate about his project, but is it realistic? Where is the audience? What are the market forces? How will it get financed?" Blind passion isn't such a great thing, after all.

We're fighting for a project now where it seems the financing will be super-difficult. It has a start date, a great cast and a lot of great things going for it. We're going to pursue it till the end, but it could go either way. Maybe we're fighting too hard if the market won't support the film.

Where do you get financing these days?

In the golden days, a decade or so ago, it seemed there were a lot of high net-worth individuals who would commit to films because they had passion for them. The person who financed *Little Miss Sunshine* was like that. He took a risk, he had no safety net, but he believed in the story. But now it seems those people are very rare.

Perhaps it's because a lot of investors lost money, so that many became "risk averse." They impose rigid business models or formulas so that only a small portion of their money is at risk. That's really too bad, because it leads to a lot of films that are made because there are the pre-sales, soft money, rebates, etc. I think if I had a billion dollars, I'd roll the dice on some films that don't make business sense but could break through because of their artistic merits. But yes, that's easy for me to say.

It does make one nostalgic for the days when you could just go to a studio like Fox or Paramount and present an interesting film, and forget the Excel spreadsheet. Some projects are just a lot better off being made with studio support. *Ruby Sparks* could have been independent, but I don't think we'd have had nearly the kind of support we did with Fox Searchlight.

Why are there now so many producer credits on so many films?

Obviously people who have a lot of money have a huge head start as producers—and probably everything else. But demanding a "produced by" credit just for making an investment doesn't seem right. They're doing it as an investment, and yet they want a credit that implies a whole different function, which they are not doing.

It's hard to say no when people make these demands in exchange for a passive investment, and that's how you end up with 20, 30 or 40 producer credits. I know that many producers rationalize this unwelcome development as "I had a moral responsibility to get my film made." But all this just trivializes the credit that the actual producers get. And in a weird way, I think it creates an embarrassing antagonism between the very necessary financiers and the active producers. I wish there were some exalted credit for financing, so that it didn't make a mockery of the producer credit yet gave respect and honor to people who took the risk and responsibility in financing the film.

Do you have a strong relationship with Sundance?

We have a long history and very positive feelings about Sundance. Michelle Satter has done a tremendous job developing and running the Sundance labs. The festival under Geoff Gilmore became a huge thing and now under John Cooper it continues to flourish. All the programmers there are really smart and know a lot about film. It's like an all-star team.

Was it an ordeal to get Nebraska *made after ten years of development?*

No, except for the wait it was a pleasure to make such a quality film without a lot of drama and anxiety. There was just a great feeling on location in Nebraska and I think the crew and the local population knew we were making a positive, emotional film. We were lucky to have the sophisticated vision of Alexander Payne as the director and the benevolent support of Paramount. The premiere of *Nebraska* in Cannes was a peak moment in our film career.

BERGER'S AND YERXA'S FILMOGRAPHY

Producer
Louder Than Bombs (2015)
Low Down (2014)
Nebraska (2013)
The Necessary Death of Charlie Countryman (2013)
Ruby Sparks (2012)
The Switch (2010)
Little Children (2006)
Little Miss Sunshine (2006)
Bee Season (2005)
The Ice Harvest (2005)
Cold Mountain (2003)
Pumpkin (2002)
The Wood (1999)

Election (1999)
King of the Hill (1993)

Executive Producer
The Leftovers—HBO (2014)
All Fall Down (documentary, 2014)
We Made This Movie (2012)
The Mexican Suitcase (2011)
Ain't In It for My Health: A Film About Levon Helm (2010)
Hamlet 2 (2008)
Chevolution (2008)
I Am Trying to Break Your Heart (documentary, 2002)
Crumb (documentary, 1994) (Berger)
Jack the Bear (1993) (Yerxa)

Clint Eastwood

A cultural icon, his heroic image projects a stoic strength to movie fans around the world. Clint Eastwood is a total filmmaker: actor, director, producer and, more recently, composer.

Eastwood formed his own production company, Malpaso, in 1968 to produce his own projects. As a producer, he has won Best Picture Oscars for Unforgiven *and* Million Dollar Baby. *He also won Best Director Oscars for those two films, as well as an Oscar nomination for Best Actor for* Million Dollar Baby. *Most recently,* American Sniper *earned an Academy Award nomination for Best Picture.*

Eastwood was honored with the Irving Thalberg Award for Lifetime Achievement by the Motion Picture Academy at the Academy Awards in 1995. He also received the American Film Institute's Lifetime Achievement Award in 1996.

During his prolific, multi-faceted career, Eastwood has produced 29 feature films, beginning with Firefox *in 1992. His latest, the box office smash* American Sniper, *garnered a Best Picture Oscar nomination and five other Academy Award nominations. Since the millennium, his producer credits also include* Space Cowboys, Blood Work, Mystic River, Flags of Our Fathers, Letters from Iwo Jima, Changeling, Gran Torino, Invictus, Hereafter, J. Edgar, Trouble with the Curve *and* Jersey Boys. *He also produced the documentary* Tony Bennett: The Music Never Ends.

Before American Sniper, Unforgiven *was his most resounding commercial success. The revisionist Western generated more than $100 million in U.S. box office and notched nine Academy Award nominations.*

In 2004 he was nominated for Oscars for Best Director and Best Picture for Mystic River, *which earned six Academy Award nominations. He earned dual Academy Award nominations in 2007 (Best Director and Best Picture) for his acclaimed World War II drama* Letters from Iwo Jima, *which tells the story of the bloody battle from the Japa-*

nese soldiers' perspective. The film won the Golden Globe and Critics' Choice Awards for Best Foreign Language Film. It also received Best Picture honors from a number of film critics groups, including the Los Angeles Film Critics Association.

Eastwood is respected and admired by various Warner Bros. executive regimes for bringing in his films on time and always under budget. The studio indulged his passion for music and offbeat material. His commercial and artistic clout allowed him to make personal films such as Bird, *based on his lifelong love for jazz.*

Eastwood first came to fame with his portrayal of cowboy Rowdy Yates on the popular TV series Rawhide. *During a summer hiatus, he hit pay dirt on the big screen in the now-legendary spaghetti Westerns* A Fistful of Dollars, For a Few Dollars More *and* The Good, the Bad and the Ugly. *At the time his decision to do a Western for Sergio Leone, an Italian director who spoke no English, in Spain was considered foolhardy.*

Eastwood was savvy and strong-minded enough to establish Malpaso early in his career. The name, taken from a creek on his property in Carmel, is ironic—it means "bad step" in Spanish. Taking charge of his career, he ventured into directing. His debut directorial effort, Play Misty for Me, *featured a startling performance by Jessica Walter and a chilling blend of music and visuals.*

His choice of roles and choices of material often went against conventional wisdom or motion picture industry advice. When he signed to play Dirty Harry, the police thriller was considered on the wane. But Eastwood's portrayal of the stoic, no-nonsense cop resonated with moviegoers and he went on to star four more times as Inspector Harry Callahan.

During the 1980s, Eastwood became a major producing force. He received his first producer credit on the aviation thriller Firefox *(1982) and followed in the same year with a haunting portrait of an alcoholic singer in* Honkytonk Man. *The other films he produced during that decade were* Sudden Impact, Tightrope, Pale Rider, Heartbreak Ridge *and* Bird.

His work was as accomplished as it was rapid-fire. He formed an informal Malpaso Road Company, a lean, fast-moving production team: production designer Henry Bumstead, editor Joel Cox, cinematographers

Bruce Surtees and Jack Green, composers Lennie Niehaus and Lalo Shifrin, and marketing-publicity men Joe Hyams and Marco Barla, and his longtime agent-manager Lennie Hirshan.

Over the course of his career, Eastwood has received many lifetime achievement honors, including the Chicago International Film Festival's Lifetime Achievement Award and the Hollywood Foreign Press Association's Cecil B. DeMille Award.

In 1991, Eastwood was Harvard's Hasty Pudding Theatrical Society's Man of the Year, and in 1992 he was honored with the California Governor's Award for the Arts. He is also the recipient of a Kennedy Center Honor and five People's Choice Awards for Favorite Motion Picture Actor. He served as president of the jury at the Cannes Film Festival in 1994. More recently, he received the Prix Lumière at the Grand Lyon Film Festival and the Commandeur de la Legion d'honneur, presented by French president Nicolas Sarkozy.

Duane Byrge: You always pull one out of nowhere. A few years back, people thought you were headed into a project on Nelson Mandela, and then you shifted gears and did Gran Torino.

Clint Eastwood: A friend of ours submitted the script for *Gran Torino* to my agent. My agent wouldn't even look at it. Anyway, they then submitted it to Rob [Lorenz]. He read it and said to me, "This script is kind of unusual. It's very politically incorrect." I said, "Let me read it."

I wasn't rushing anything. I liked the story about this guy in the Rust Belt who can't fathom all the change. I felt right with *Gran Torino*, so we just did it then. It was the same sort of deal with *Trouble with the Curve*, which was a script that Rob got from a friend. I thought these baseball movies normally don't do much, but it was a nice father-daughter love story. I thought it was worth telling.

A movie is storytelling. You can tell any kind of story. It doesn't have to be a story that I've lived through or even have any sort of statement. Sometimes that just comes out in the movie. Take a film like *Million Dollar Baby*—I wasn't just anxious to do a boxing movie, especially a lady boxing movie. I liked the relationship and the surrogate father-daughter dynamic, and the fact that he never knew his own daughter. He was the father that she never had. It's human relationships that make a story worth telling.

There are a lot of pictures that don't have any of that. I've done some also that don't have that. Sometimes the family unit has a big thing to do with a story, like *Bronco Billy* or *The Outlaw Josey Wales*. Those kinds of extended family stories have appeal.

What about J. Edgar?

I grew up with Hoover and G-men. I knew there were all these various positions on him. Having read all these different books over the years, I was always trying to find out more about him. Hoover is interesting. When the Japanese-Americans were interred in World War II, Hoover was against that. He came out against Roosevelt and the Secretary of State. So, he had ideas that were varied, more independent in some ways. But he was paranoid about espionage, and, in some cases, such as the Rosenbergs, he was right.

I grew up in the whole era of the Cold War and espionage, and the Rosenbergs trial. Many people were saying, "They're being railroaded." When the Cold War ended, the KGB for a period was allowed to open their files, and we found out the Rosenbergs were guilty. So you start speculating: "Let's see... If the Soviets hadn't gotten the hydrogen bomb as early as they did because there was no espionage involved, there wouldn't have been a Korean War. Stalin and the Russians wanted to back North Korea, but they wouldn't have done that if they didn't have atomic weaponry. There wouldn't have been a Vietnam War, probably." You think of all the people who would have been alive now if they hadn't gotten that information.

You don't link "Clint Eastwood" with "Broadway musical." Now you are doing Jersey Boys. How did that come about?

I'll try anything, as long as I like the material and as long as I like the characters. If you have good character development, I'm interested. With *Jersey Boys*, Graham King called here. He asked if we would be interested in doing it. So they shipped it over. I read the script. Then I found out there were other scripts, and I read all the scripts. I finally found one that I thought was good.

Also, I liked the music. I think that "Too Good to Be True, Can't Take My Eyes Off of You" is one of the few classic songs that came out of that era. That song could have been written in the days of Cole

Porter, Johnny Mercer. A lot of rock 'n' roll is more frivolous—"I love short shorts," that kind of thing.

Almost everybody that we've cast in the picture has played the role in one of the productions. I've kind of cherry-picked from the various productions. I've got guys from the Broadway production, from the San Francisco production, from Las Vegas, all over. All of them have done it before, so it should be easy. We just cast Christopher Walken as the old gangster. It should be an easy shoot, mostly in clubs here in L.A. and some in New Jersey.

You remind me of Bronco Billy. You are always putting on a new show, and you're always enthused about it.

You just try things. You never know where a story comes from. One day Morgan Freeman said to me, "Here's a script on Mandela." Well, I was always interested in him as a character. The script had an athletic storyline about the South African rugby team. Well, I knew that no one over here is really interested in rugby, but you go ahead and try it anyway.

Clint Eastwood., c. 2014. Courtesy Malpaso Prods.

What is your idea of a producer?

Well, there are certain types. Hal Wallis and Dick Zanuck, people like that in the studio days. They knew a lot about movies. Those kinds of guys were real producers. They did everything.

Today, you could be a guy who just financed the project, or put some money behind the writer. Or you could be somebody who likes the entire process and has some ideas about casting. I think you can be all of those things. At the same time, there are people who are friends with the leading actor, and their credit is in there because they lent him $10 in 1980.

What led you to producing?

Being an actor, there are two mindsets. Some people reach a certain success being an actor and they think that's great. They just want to expand on that and play certain roles. And others become interested in the whole moviemaking mechanism. I'm just a curious kind of guy. I guess that's what's led me to it.

I founded Malpaso back in '68 and really got active in production. At the time, I was doing a couple of big pictures with a lot of extras, like *Paint Your Wagon*. That could have been a decent picture—it just got so big—there was no way to control it. It didn't have the leadership it could have had. They were all talented people. There just wasn't management.

As a producer you are well regarded for not letting anything get out of hand. One of your company's first productions was **Thunderbolt and Lightfoot,** *directed by Michael Cimino. His next film was* **Heaven's Gate.**

Sometimes people get into a picture or halfway into it, and everybody's afraid to intercede. So, they just let it go. A picture was supposed to cost maybe $20 million, and it ends up costing $100 million. How did that happen?

When we did *Thunderbolt and Lightfoot*, Mike was young and hungry. He wanted to do the job. We surrounded him with good people and everything. I always got along great with him. Some other people, I guess, had a rough time expressing themselves. Or saying, "Okay, this is going crazy, and we've got to do something about this." Back in the studio days, when the movie industry was run by guys like Darryl Zanuck, Harry Cohn, Jack L. Warner, they wouldn't let people just go crazy.

Do you regret not being around when the studio system thrived in the '30s and '40s?

Selfishly, I like it the way it is now because we make the films, and everybody stays out of the way. I wouldn't want them to stay out of the way if I needed help, or if I was running off and doing something that was not right. I have a certain price, I guess.

I think this is a good time, even though I do have admiration for those guys. I've always regretted not working with Anthony Mann, Hawks, Sturges—I would love to have worked on some of those movies. I worked with Bill Wellman, a few of them, but that's all.

You keep on budget, ahead of schedule. That's a sign of a dependable producer.

Over the years people say, "He comes in on budget all the time." I always thought nobody really gives a damn if you are ten weeks over. Nobody really cares about anybody being thrifty. I remember getting a bonus for saving money. If a person has enough faith to finance a picture, I owe them the best attention that it's not going to cost more. There's a lavishness that sometimes gets out of hand in movies.

Is it because of intense preparation that you don't have the logistical problems?

You just do what you think is right at the time. I'm sure somebody could else come along and do it differently. You just develop your own style after a while, your own thoughts about acting, directing, about production, your own philosophies. There are all kinds of ways to do things—as long as you end up with a good product at the end. Everyone has the same desires for a project to be good, it's just how you get there.

There are no experts, and there are a lot of people who think they are, but they really aren't. I'm no expert. I just do what I like. Make things that I'd like to see.

Still, everybody is trying to pigeonhole everything. Even after you do upwards of 30 films, you still have trouble expanding. With *Million Dollar Baby*, the studio took it apprehensively. They thought it was a boxing picture. To me, it was a love story. You have two lost people: the father she didn't have, and the daughter he didn't have a relationship with.

You never know. Sure as hell down the road, someone will say, "Who wants to see that?" Even after we completed *Million Dollar Baby*, the studio liked it, but they still weren't sure what it was. I talked with

[Warner Bros. executive] Danny Feldman. He asked me, "Why don't we just put it out, in a couple theaters?" I said. "Let's do that, and see what it does." So he put it out there in around five theaters in London, New York, L.A. and Chicago. It turned out that it captured the imagination of the audience.

Unforgiven, *which won you the Oscar for Best Picture, almost didn't make it to the screen.*

Unforgiven turned out to be a favorite of mine. It turned out to be my biggest Western script. And to this day, I've never seen another one like that. It's why I've never done another one.

Unforgiven had been submitted here in 1979 or 1980. Sonia Chernus, who was the reader for me at the time, hated it. She showed me her critique, so I didn't read the script. A year or so later, somebody else was preparing it—Francis Coppola. He had kind of run into a stalemate. At the time a reader for Warner Bros. said to me, "You ought to read this script from this writer. [The] script isn't available, but you ought to read it for the writer."

So I read it, and I really liked it. I called up the agent. I just wanted to see if the writer had anything else in his pocket. I really liked his writing. The agent said that it was available. It was just the day after Coppola had let it go.

I called [Warner Bros. executive] Terry Semel. The script was called *The William Money Killings.* I said, "Terry, what's the story on this? You didn't like it?"

He said, "Oh. no, we liked it, but we thought Coppola's budget was a little too high." Well, I said, "I love it, and it's available." He said, "If you want to do it, we'll go there."

It's ironic how things fall into place. There was a similar thing on *The Outlaw Josey Wales.* It was a book by Whippoorwill Publishing in Arkansas. I never heard of it. Its cover was really terrible. It was hardcover, but looked like a comic book. It was called *The Rebel Outlaw Josey Wales.* It sat on my desk for a while. I just let it sit there.

We found out that Whippoorwill Publishing had only published 75 copies of it. Bob Daly, who was working for me here then, picked it up. He was a prolific reader and a bachelor. Every night he would read over dinner. So he said, "I'll take it and read it tonight." The next morning he came in and said, "I couldn't put it down." I said, "Let me take a look at it." I took the horrible cover off, so I didn't have to look at that. I started reading it, and I couldn't put it down. I read it in one reading.

So, I called the [author]. The guy was down in Oklahoma somewhere—Forrest Carter—and he had written one or two books. So we went ahead right away. It was the first picture I did when I moved into this office at Warner Bros., after I had come over from Universal. There have been a lot of crazy things that come like that over the years just out of the woodwork. You just never know where a good project is going to come from.

You don't have a wall of staff people cutting things off?

We have a wall. My agent hated *Every Which Way but Loose*. My lawyer hated it. They hated it, but I wanted to do it. I told them, "It's a family movie, not R-rated, and I think it has got some good craziness to it." The fact that the guy loses the fight, loses the girl. It was just kind of crazy.

The same thing with *The Changeling*. My agent said, "This isn't something you would want to do." I know Ron Howard and Brian Grazer, who had submitted it here. Out of courtesy to them, I started reading. I couldn't put it down.

I hate to think how many scripts I might have lost along the way because somebody else turned it down. If you don't follow your instincts, and you rely on somebody else's opinion, you may win a few, but you are going to lose a few.

Everybody has a story. Every studio has those pictures that they let get away. Universal turned down *Star Wars*. Here they turned down *Home Alone*. Every studio has their history like that, a few things where they made some mistakes, and a few things where they've been successful.

But you've always had the producer part of you, always searching for a project. Early on you made things happen. With Play Misty for Me, you brought it along to the point where you became a director.

It had been given to me by a girl I knew who wrote it. She was working as a legal secretary and hadn't written a lot of things. She had this little 50-page deal. I took an option on it for a year. I gave her five or ten grand. It was pretty expensive at the time.

Then I went off and made *Where Eagles Dare*. While I was making *Where Eagles Dare*, she called me up and said, "I've got an opportunity to sell this thing, and I really need the dough." She told me that Ross Hunter wanted to buy it. I said, "Well, okay, I can't do anything now. I'm stuck over here for quite a while." And then I had no guarantee I could even put it together, because it was only a 50-page treatment at that point.

So, I let it go. And I came back and went off and did *Paint Your Wagon*, and that's another six months, then *The Beguiled*. One time when I was in [Lew] Wasserman's office, putting *The Beguiled* together, I told him that there was a project I always liked, but that Ross Hunter was going to do it. I asked him what had happened to it. "Well," he said, "it's kind of on the shelf now."

"Well, if it ever comes off the shelf, I'd like to do it." So, then I went off and did *The Beguiled*. Finally he said, "It's off the shelf, you can have it." So I got it and asked Dean Reisner to re-write it, since it wasn't in script form. I figured I could change it from L.A. to Carmel, and go home and do it there. We made it for $700,000.

And since you were now the producer, you could suggest yourself as director.

That was the other part. I told Lew Wasserman, "Not only do I want to do it. I'd like to direct it." And he said, without even batting an eye, "Okay." That was great, something I've always wanted to do. I'm walking down the hallway and Wasserman calls out and grabs my agent—I had a multi-picture deal with them as an actor and I was getting a fairly good price at the time as an actor. The agent comes over to me and says, "They don't want to pay you what they'd pay you on your actor's fee, but they have to pay minimum."

"Okay, they shouldn't even be paying me," I said. "I should be paying them. I should have to show them something in order to direct."

You were a smart producer—you got yourself cheap as director.

59

Most people are always bitching about pay. My dad was always an advocate of the work ethic thing: work for nothing, show them what you've got, and make yourself valuable. I had that drummed into me since I was about five years old. So, there I was. One thing led to another. Here I am 45 years later, still doing this.

You're getting better.

I hope so. Everybody should get better at everything, if they allow themselves. Too many people stay in a comfort zone. Why upset the apple cart? I was always taking chances, jumping off the bridge.

If you look back on it, everything you do in life is kind of a fluke. To do *A Fistful of Dollars* was kind of a fluke. I was on hiatus from doing a TV western [*Rawhide*]. I didn't want to go do a Western in Spain. But William Morris said they promised their office in Rome that I would take a look at it. So, I took it home and, of course, it turned out to be a spin-off of one of my favorite Kurosawa movies. I got all stoked up.

That would have changed the whole trajectory of your career?

Who knows what would have happened? Maybe nothing. Maybe I'd be in a TV series somewhere. One thing led to another. When people ask me about how you become an actor, a director, producer—it works that way. There you are, and all of a sudden, the chain of events starts falling into place.

When I left Sergio, he wanted me to do *Once Upon a Time in the West*. I just said, "Nah. After doing *The Good, the Bad and the Ugly*, that's fine by me." It was time to move on. I came back and started doing pictures here. Picking the times when to leave and when to go—that's important. You have to put yourself out there. Otherwise you're putting the block up for yourself. I do crazy things, all along the way. You've got to jump into the pool. It's kind of like Newman and Redford jumping off the cliff in *Butch Cassidy and the Sundance Kid*. There is no way you are going to climb down.

You did stick around for the Dirty Harry sequels.

There is the temptation to stay with a franchise. People still ask me, "Do you ever think you'll do another *Dirty Harry*?" I'm over 80 years old. They wouldn't let an old guy like me be on the police force.

Dirty Harry would be retired. He would be sitting there at the VFW or the Elks Club.

But here's how you'd do it. You go into a little beer bar in some small town. There would be this guy with the gray hair on a stool, and it's Dirty Harry. He's just sitting there. These guys come in and order a bunch of beers, and they say, "Hand over all your money" or something like that. Then, you cut to Dirty Harry. And, with his history, you know what he is going to do [*laughs*]. So, you don't have to make the movie, you just make the short.

As a producer, you are involved all through the marketing and release pattern.

In the marketing of *Thunderbolt and Lightfoot*, we were sitting here and they had two ads. One was a good one. It was a little different. And the other one was just stupid action stuff. The ad guy said they'd run the good one in the *New York Times*, and the other one they'd run in the *Post*.

I asked why. They said that the working-class guy is not going to like the good ad. And I said, "Really?" I looked out the window and I saw a bunch of guys lifting this piano out of a truck out there. I said, "Hang on a second." I gave it to Judy from our office and said, "Take this over and show these two ads to these guys, and tell me which one they like." She came back, and said they liked the good one.

You can't treat the audience like they're stupid or look down on them. Everybody has ideas. Just give them a chance to express themselves. They might not have earned their Ph.D., but they've learned their business. They've been through the education of life. Everybody is capable of being a Ph.D. in life, if you open yourself to it.

When I make a movie I hope the janitor likes it, and I hope the head of the company likes it. You have no control over that anyway. You have to make what you like. And you have to believe in it yourself. When you're done, you have to be able to say, "That's the way I wanted it." If it does succeed with the audience, you say, "Isn't that terrific?" If it doesn't, you can still say, "I'm proud of it. It didn't work."

If you like the stories, you do it. On *Mystic River*, when I was completing it in the post-production period, *Million Dollar Baby* came along. It was a story I'd read three or four years earlier, but now it was in a screenplay. I liked it, so I said, "All right, we'll start that." Normally, I take a little down time. Have five or six months between projects. Those two were right there. I said, "We'll do them while the dice are hot."

When I was preparing *Flags of Our Fathers*, I was in a meeting with [Steven] Spielberg, and I said, "I want to try something. I want to see if I can get a screenplay on the other side. Just to see what those poor Japanese kids went through. They didn't want to be there. They were shipped over there by their government and told they were never coming back." How the hell do you deliver that kind of mentality? Americans would not fathom that.

I told [*Flags of Our Fathers* screenwriter] Paul Haggis that I didn't have the dough to pay him to write that screenplay. I asked him if he had a student or somebody he knew who could maybe do a spec. A couple of days later he called back and said that he found this young woman who was Japanese-American and a good student, a good researcher. She went on spec, and she ended up writing a good script. It became one of my favorites.

When I went to Iceland to shoot the stuff with Iwo Jima for *Flags*, I told the script supervisor to put down in her notes "other project." I did various shots. There were a couple of them that had Japanese actors we had gotten from the Air Force base. So, I said, "We'll just bank it." I left Iceland with all the stuff for *Flags*, but also had six or seven shots for *Iwo Jima*.

While we were doing post-production on *Flags*, we flew over to Iwo Jima and started laying it out with a script, the whole deal. Bill Ireton, who was the head of Warners in Japan, got me all the information and got me approvals from the mayor of Tokyo—Iwo Jima is in his jurisdiction. The mayor went for it. I met him, and it turned out he was a writer and liked movies. I told him I wanted to do it from Japanese soldiers' point of view. In Japan, it was odd because they had ignored that battle of Iwo Jima. None of the actors had ever heard of it. These Japanese actors, 21 or 22 years old, didn't know anything about Iwo Jima.

So we went over there and convinced them we would do a great job on it if we could shoot some on Iwo. We said we'd do nothing radical, and that we would do a good job. We just put it together like that.

We got a silver mine up by Barstow, which was wonderful for the shoot. We brought all the Japanese actors over. None of them spoke English, and their big thrill was to go to Las Vegas one weekend when we weren't shooting.

One thing fell into another. Here I am in post-production on one picture and I'm shooting another. That's the producer part of me, always looking. It was an interesting feeling of going to Iceland and knowing you had a nice script on the other side.

That's pretty much what you did while releasing Jersey Boys. ***You moved right into*** American Sniper.

American Sniper was an interesting project. It came to me very quickly. The studio was bouncing back and forth on it. I knew that Spielberg was doing it, and I was just reading it on my own for pleasure. The studio called me and said, "They're not doing it now. Would you like to do it?"

I said, "Let me finish the book. I've got about 30 pages left, and I'll call you back." I finished it and called them and said that I could do it. This was right on the heels of *Jersey Boys.* It was back to back. In fact, I was just doing the release of *Jersey Boys* when they approached me with *American Sniper.*

They sent over a screenplay and we went from there. I liked the part of the script that accentuated the horrors of war and the effects it has on the soldiers and their families. I liked that human part, rather than just making a straight shoot-'em-up. And the personal sides of Chris Kyle and how he dealt with it all, with what we used to call "shell shock," but now they've got names for it, post-traumatic stress disorder and so on. I told the studio, "I'd like to have a meeting with the writer, Jason Hall, and ask him some questions on where he's going." It didn't have an ending so we had to add an ending.

How about casting?

Bradley Cooper was connected with the project before I came in, but I thought he'd do a great job, and he did. One of the great scenes was his awkwardness when the soldier approached him in the store and told him that he had saved his life. When we first did the scene, I wasn't sure how that was going to play, but Bradley had talked to the writer about Kyle's embarrassment. Rather than treating it like an "old pal" thing, he was trying to take the attention off himself. He started talking to the guy's kid.

The rest of the casting I did. I went down to Texas and met [Kyle's wife] Taya and got an idea of what kind of person she was. Sienna Miller came in and did a reading for the part—we had numerous young ladies come in and do that—but her reading was quite outstanding. And she also had the same sort of attitude that Taya had.

You composed a very moving theme for her in the movie. I guess Eastwood the producer is always looking to Eastwood the composer. I recall the terrific, lilting musical theme you contributed in The Bridges of Madison County. *Music plays a big part in your movies.* American Sniper *had one of the most moving trumpet solos at the end.*

Well, on this one our composer, Ennio Morricone, deserves all the credit. Over 50 years ago, when I was doing *The Good, the Bad and the Ugly*, Sergio Leone played me this record. It was called "Silencio." He was considering it for *The Good, the Bad and the Ugly*. To make a long story short, he ended up getting Ennio Morricone to write the music for *The Good, the Bad and the Ugly*, and it's one of *the* great movie scores. Amazingly, more than 50 years later, we were able to get Ennio Morricone to do our score. So back then, they didn't use "Silencio" *for The Good, the Bad and the Ugly*, but I remembered it and thought we could cut our score to this theme.

It had been so long ago that I had heard it, but I always remembered it. I tried to track it down, got all the reading material on it. It took about two or three weeks. Every day I'd come in to work and I'd say to Rob Lorenz, "Have you found that music?" One day, he came up and told me he had found it with RCA Records. I said, "Go and buy it for us." In the movie, the song you're referring to is called "The Funeral."

When American Sniper *was released, the movie sparked a flurry of criticism and controversy from such people as Michael Moore.*

I don't care about Michael Moore or anybody else who wants to bring in controversy. The press would ask me, "Well, what do you think about Michael Moore's comments?" I just said, "Maybe he's right. He's got his ideas, and he's made himself a bit of a name doing that, so, what the hell?"

You're always on to the next one, when everybody assumes you're resting up from the last one. What's on deck?
I am just finishing a movie on Chesley Sullenberger, the pilot who successfully landed the U.S. Airways plane in the Hudson River in 2009. A friend of mine, Allyn Stewart, was involved with it. She had been working on it for some time with a writer, Todd Komarnicki. Kristina, my assistant here, liked it, and she passed it around. The others liked it, and I liked it. So, we were all kind of in on the decision-making. It's just titled *Sully*. We've just finished with shooting and are now in post production.

Ever been with a project that seemed to be dead and then you got it going again?
Bridges of Madison County was like that. Spielberg's company had the project and they brought it to Warner's. They came and asked me to act in it. They got a director [Bruce Beresford] who brought in another writer, who went off on a whole other tangent.

Richard LaGravenese had written the first script, and I didn't think it was that bad, and Spielberg didn't think it was that bad. But everybody else didn't like it. The director didn't like it. He was either partial to his own writer or didn't see it from that approach.

I always liked LaGravenese's script because it took the woman's point of view. The book was written from the guy's point of view. You follow him along in this truck, and he's got his photography stuff and his cases of beer. We figured it should be from her point of view, since she's the one who has the big dramatic decision to make about her life.

It was a project that was falling apart. Warner Bros asked me to come in. We had a little contention on how it should be made. The prior administration had decided to build bridges. They said you can't film at the bridges. I said, "Who says so?" I said, "No, you talk to the historical guy and how we want to be true to the story and feature the bridges. We want to protect them, and we'll make a donation to their bridges society." Sure enough, they said, "Go ahead."

The studio had decided to build bridges at hundreds of thousands of dollars. Art directors love to build stuff. I said you didn't have to do that. We went there with a little donation and a promise to them we'd restore any bridges they wanted. We wouldn't do anything they didn't want done to them.

One of the reasons they said why we would have to build our own bridges was that there was no light in the bridges, and they won't let you take light. I said, "How about just knocking a panel here and there, and the light will come in? It will give you a very interesting dapple lighting all the way through." Well, they said, you can't. I said, "Sure you can. Tell the guy in Iowa. Make him a part of it. You promise them that everything goes back exactly as it was, and better if they want it better, but not better if they don't want it better." It's just a question of a little bit of salesmanship. It's not b.s.-ing anybody. It's just living up to your promise. That is the producer part. Otherwise, no one was going to step forward. That is part of what a producer does.

It sounds like you and Steven Spielberg willed the project into being.

Spielberg was over in the Hamptons, and I was up at Mount Shasta. So, I'd write scenes at night and fax them over to him. He'd critique it, write stuff and make changes. We were faxing back and forth. Finally, we had it done.

So I called up Richard LaGravenese, and said we were going back to his script. I told him that Steven and I had been screwing around with it awhile. He said, "That's great, but I'd love to take one more pass. Would you mind?" I said, "No, go ahead. Here it is." So he did. He cleaned up a few things, and we went with it.

You've worked with the same team over the years. You tend to use a lot of the same crew members—a veteran group that can move immediately, turn on a dime.

I guess that's why I stayed with the same guys. Henry [Bumstead] all through his later years kept telling me, "You should be using a young guy." I'd say, "But Henry, it's nice having somebody older than me around."

What's your least favorite part of the process?

There are those little things that you've just got to do, especially if I'm in the project. They're always fiddling with my collar. I've always got somebody fiddling with me all the time, but you just have to do it. Things like wardrobe, trying on shoes. That kind of thing. If you have good people around you, and it's a happy set, it will work out fine.

As a producer, you've even cast yourself in the music. You're making a name as a composer.

Well, I write music. I'm usually inspired to do that by the cutting. Looking at the cuts. I go home at night, maybe put it on a synthesizer. The next day I bring it in, and Joel [Cox] will put it on. One thing leads to another.

In some cases, I've had somebody write the parts to it. Sometimes I'd just play the piano, and Lennie [Niehaus] would come in and write the strings. And then he'd write all the high stuff. On *Unforgiven* I wrote the theme on the way to location. I was stopped off in Idaho for a couple days, and I started fiddling with the piano. And I said, "This sounds like this movie." I played it for Meryl [Streep] and said, "This reminds me of you. What do you think?" She liked it. I even specified the guitar player, Laurindo Almeida. He's the guy I wanted to play it. He just had that haunting, simple thing. I told him, "Make it like you don't know how to play as well as you do."

That's ultimate producing: You get the sound of it, and then you choose the guitar player who will get just the right sound.

Yeah, it's kind of like you're casting all the time for every part of the movie. You cast the crew when you shoot the picture. You want a crew that is compatible with your thoughts. You cast your musicians. You cast everything—it's not just casting actors. That could be the producer's job or the director's job, depending on how involved the producer is or the director is.

What about technology?

I think the technology now is great, but only if you don't let the toys run the store. I was talking to Spielberg once, and he was lamenting [the end of the era in which] you touched the film when you were editing. I work on Avid [a revolutionary non-linear digital editing system introduced in 1989] but I still remember those days. Avid can be really fast, but if you are not really decisive, it can be slower. Same with visual effects, you can do so many things.

I love the technology I resisted at first. I resisted digital intermediates for a while. After you shot the film, you put it digitally. Now I like it and I was able to go back with *Dirty Harry*, the original one. I thought there were flaws in it. The blood makeup, it was too much like paint. It was almost orange. With the digital, I could go back and darken. During the digital intermediate, we could change the density. It was just kind of amazing.

We showed it at the Directors Guild. It was the first time I had seen it on the big screen since 1971. I'll tell you it looked pretty good after going through this process. We couldn't have done that without the technology of today.

With some technology, I'm still a little slow. I don't use computers now very much. I never have my cell phone on. It's always for transmitting, not for receiving. Even with new technology and everything, I think producing is just good logical decisions. It is nothing more than being logical in trying to express a thought. I don't think there is any brain surgery to it. You're dealing with a certain amount of information you've acquired over 50 years, and you kind of remember things that seemed logical and things that seemed illogical.

Even when you are working with a bad producer or director, it's a good experience because you are learning what not to do. I'd just make note of it, and make sure I'd never do that. It's all just trial and error.

EASTWOOD'S FILMOGRAPHY

Producer
Sully (2016)
American Sniper (2014)
Jersey Boys (2014)
Trouble with the Curve (2012)
J. Edgar (2011)
Hereafter (2010)
Invictus (2009)
Gran Torino (2008)

Changeling (2008)
Tony Bennett: The Music Never Ends (2007)
Letters from Iwo Jima (2006)
Flags of Our Fathers (2006)
Million Dollar Baby (2004)
Mystic River (2003)
Blood Work (2002)
Space Cowboys (2000)

True Crime (1999)
Midnight in the Garden of Good and Evil (1997)
Absolute Power (1997)
The Stars Fell on Henrietta (1995)
The Bridges of Madison County (1995)
A Perfect World (1993)
Unforgiven (1992)
White Hunter Black Heart (1990)
Bird (1988)
Heartbreak Ridge (1986)
Pale Rider (1985)
Tightrope (1984)
Sudden Impact (1983)
Honkytonk Man (1982)
Firefox (1982)

Director
Sully (2016)
American Sniper (2014)
Jersey Boys (2014)
J. Edgar (2011)
Hereafter (2010)
Invictus (2009)
Gran Torino (2008)
Changeling (2008)
Letters from Iwo Jima (2006)
Flags of Our Fathers (2006)

Million Dollar Baby (2004)
Mystic River (2003)
Blood Work (2002)
Space Cowboys (2000)
True Crime (1999)
Midnight in the Garden of Good and Evil (1997)
Absolute Power (1997)
The Bridges of Madison County (1995)
A Perfect World (1993)
Unforgiven (1992)
The Rookie (1990)
White Hunter Black Heart (1990)
Bird (1988)
Heartbreak Ridge (1986)
Pale Rider (1985)
Sudden Impact (1983)
Honkytonk Man (1982)
Firefox (1982)
Bronco Billy (1980)
The Gauntlet (1977)
The Outlaw Josey Wales (1976)
The Eiger Sanction (1975)
Breezy (1973)
High Plains Drifter (1973)
Play Misty for Me (1971)

Taylor Hackford

A director who became a producer to protect his artistic vision, Taylor Hackford rose to filmmaking fame when he directed An Officer and a Gentleman *(1982). Starring Richard Gere and Debra Winger,* Officer *(Hackford's second film) became a commercial and critical hit and received six Oscar nominations (supporting actor Louis Gossett Jr. and the song "Up Where We Belong" were winners). Hackford was nominated by the Directors Guild of America for his outstanding achievement.*

Hackford has functioned as both director and producer on his subsequent films. His credits include Against All Odds, *starring Jeff Bridges, Rachel Ward and James Woods;* White Nights, *starring Mikhail Baryshnikov, Gregory Hines, Helen Mirren and Isabella Rossellini;* Everybody's All-American, *starring Dennis Quaid, Jessica Lange and John Goodman; and the documentary* Chuck Berry Hail! Hail! Rock 'n' Roll, *featuring Chuck Berry and Keith Richards.*

In 2005, Hackford completed a 15-year quest to make the life story of Ray Charles, Ray. *He directed, produced and co-wrote the worldwide hit. The film was nominated for six Academy Awards, including Best Director and Best Picture. It won two Oscars: one for Jamie Foxx as Best Actor and another for Best Sound. The film's soundtrack won two Grammy Awards.*

Hackford grew up in Santa Barbara and went to the University of Southern California on a Trustee Scholarship. Following graduation he served as a Peace Corps volunteer in Bolivia, where he learned to speak Spanish and to appreciate Latino culture. In 1969 he began his entertainment career at KCET, the Los Angeles public television affiliate, where he pioneered the presentation of uninterrupted rock 'n' roll performances on American TV. In addition to creating several award-winning documentaries for the station's cultural department, he also served as an investigative reporter in their news division. He received an Associated Press Award, a Peabody and two Emmys.

70

In 1978 he left KCET to begin a filmmaking career. His first effort was a short film, Teenage Father, *which he wrote, produced and directed. He won an Academy Award for Best Documentary Short Subject.*

The "realistic" tone of Teenage Father, *plus Hackford's extensive music résumé, impressed the producers of* The Idolmaker *who hired him to write and direct. Set in the world of pop music, the film was about the making and managing of two early '60s "Teenage Idol" rock stars.*

Hackford's love of music has played an important part in his career. His films have generated three Gold albums and two Platinum albums, as well as six singles that reached #1 on the Billboard Singles Charts. As a director-producer he had five #1 songs in consecutive films.

Hackford has been fascinated by all things Latino since his stint as a Peace Corp volunteer in South America in 1968 and '69. In the 1970s, outside the Hollywood system, Hackford and his friend Daniel Valdez conceived a film on the life of Ritchie Valens with Valdez playing the title role. At the time, neither had the credibility or clout to get the project made. However, after the success of An Officer and a Gentleman *and* Against All Odds, *Hackford was able to develop* La Bamba, *the Ritchie Valens biography. Wanting the project to have an authentic Latino pedigree, he hired Daniel Valdez's brother Luis to write the script, and when Columbia gave the project a green light, tapped Luis to direct the film. Since Daniel Valdez was now too old to play the title role, the producers found an unknown, Lou Diamond Phillips, to play Valens.* La Bamba *became a sleeper success, breaking new ground for Hispanic artists in Hollywood.*

While Hackford was producing La Bamba, *he shot the musical documentary* Chuck Berry Hail! Hail! Rock 'n' Roll, *which garnered him some of the best reviews of his career. Collaborating with Keith Richards of the Rolling Stones, Hackford revealed the dark side of Berry, the brilliant, thorny genius who many consider the most important and talented figure in the birth of rock 'n' roll.*

In 1988, Hackford merged New Visions with production-distribution company New Century Entertainment. He became chairman and CEO of New Century/New Visions, which produced five modestly budgeted movies with other directors. New Vision releases include The Long Walk Home, Mortal Thoughts, Defenseless *and* Queens Logic.

In 1992, Hackford returned to directing, helming the crime drama, Blood In, Blood Out *(Bound by Honor). This film brought him a Best Director nod from the 1993 Tokyo International Film Festival. His next film, the horror-thriller* Dolores Claiborne *starring Kathy Bates and Jennifer Jason Leigh, was selected for screening at the 1995 Venice, Deauville and Tokyo Film Festivals.*

In 1996 Hackford discovered some unreleased documentary footage of the legendary 1974 Muhammad Ali–George Foreman "Rumble in the Jungle" title fight in Zaire, Africa. Hackford restructured the footage, combining it with present-day interviews with Norman Mailer, George Plimpton, Spike Lee, et al., and footage of the original fight to create a feature-length documentary, When We Were Kings. *It was a hit at the 1996 Sundance Film Festival and won the 1997 Academy Award for Best Documentary Feature.*

In 1998 Hackford directed and executive-produced the worldwide hit The Devil's Advocate *(1999), a contemporary morality tale starring Al Pacino and Keanu Reeves. In 2001 he produced and directed* Proof of Life *with Meg Ryan, Russell Crowe and David Morse, based on William Prochnau's* Vanity Fair *article "Adventures in the Ransom Trade," about the real-life kidnapping of American businessman Thomas Hargrove.*

In 2005 Hackford completed his 15-year quest to bring the life of Ray Charles to the screen when Ray *became an international hit. Hackford's* Love Ranch *(2010), starring Helen Mirren and Joe Pesci, focused on a husband-wife team opening the first legal brothel in Nevada.*

Taylor's most recent feature film Parker *(2013), an action-crime drama adapted from a novel by Donald Westlake, starred Jason Stathem and Jennifer Lopez. More recently, Hackford bankrolled his first stage production,* Louis & Keely: Live at the Sahara, *based on the lives of the husband-and-wife musical team Louie Prima and Keely Smith. The production ran at the Geffen Playhouse.*

Duane Byrge: Your background and education would not lead anyone to guess that you would become a movie producer. How did your path lead to Hollywood?

Taylor Hackford: I wasn't one of those people who grew up in a movie theater. I was raised working class in Santa Barbara. My mother was a waitress, but although there wasn't much money, I took advantage of the gifts of Southern California coastal life. I had good friends—Ron Shelton [*Bull Durham*] and I were in the same graduating class. We played basketball together.

I studied hard and won a Trustee Scholarship to go to USC, which is an expensive school. I majored in International Relations. I've always been political, and this was the late '60s, Vietnam, so there was tremendous ferment. I ran for student body president of USC and got elected. SC had always been a politically conservative school, but I was able to shake things up a bit: introducing the first student evaluation of the faculty, starting a student cooperative book store, getting SC to join the National Student Association.

The USC Division of Cinema was beginning to take off at that time. George Lucas and John Milius were there in the mid '60s.

I never took a film class, but I started to hang with film students in my senior year and watch films with them. The Cinema School was in a little bungalow next to the tennis courts. For the first time in my life, I started really looking at film seriously.

Taylor Hackford, c. 2014. Courtesy Taylor Hackford.

I graduated in '67, right at the height of the political and social rebellion. I was accepted into SC's law school, but Vietnam was going on and I would have been drafted. I decided to do alternative service and joined the Peace Corps. I also got married to my high school sweetheart who had gone to Sarah Lawrence. We went to Bolivia together as Peace Corps volunteers. While I was in South America, I started rethinking my future. I had been bitten by the film bug, and was particularly focused on the power of film to change people's hearts and minds politically. We were living in a barrio above La Paz, so I was close enough to be able to go down into the city on weekends to see movies. My wife and I were pretty much hippies, and the movies we wanted to see were mostly European. Lucky for us, that's what was playing in La Paz.

My wife and I came back to the U.S. in 1969, a rather propitious time. Falling back on my original plans, I enrolled in law school, but almost immediately I realized that my direction had changed. After two weeks I got up and walked out of class, forfeiting my tuition money … the only money I had. I needed to find a job quick in order to support my family—my wife had just become pregnant. I remembered that when I was student body president at SC, I had participated in a TV discussion at KCET, the Public Broadcasting Station in Los Angeles. Not having any other contacts in the film-media business, I went to KCET and asked for a job. Luckily, the producer of Public Affairs remembered me and recommended me for a job. The only job available was delivering mail, so I took it.

During the day I was delivering mail and running a printing press, but at night I started going to classic American and European films. Luckily my pregnant wife liked film, so we'd attend 14 films a week. I also bought a Super 8 camera and, on the weekends, started putting my ideas on film.

After six months, I worked my way out of the mailroom, becoming a political reporter and cultural affairs producer. I covered City Hall and the Hall of Administration during the day, I also started contributing to the station's cultural department in the evening, pushing KCET to open its programming to include rock music. It did and before commercial TV woke up to this new cultural explosion with shows like *In Concert* and *Midnight Special*, KCET pioneered uninterrupted rock 'n' roll on television. We actually did the first rock 'n' roll simulcasts in the country, with artists like Cat Stevens and Leon Russell.

So you had become a producer.
In public television, the creative person was the producer—the one who controls a program, comes up with the idea, writes it and shoots it. I was having a ball. KCET became my film school. They were understaffed but had actual airtime to fill. As long as you didn't screw up and didn't mind working around the clock, you had a fantastic opportunity to work in several genres simultaneously. I've never been lazy, so this job was a godsend to me. I won two Associated Press awards for my journalism, and our nightly news show won a Peabody Award. My documentary about L.A. poet Charles Bukowski won the CPB Award as the best Cultural Program on PBS, and also received the Silver Reel at the San Francisco Film Festival.

Meanwhile, our music programs were being picked up nationally on the PBS network. This recognition gave the management confidence, and they asked for something more ambitious about Los Angeles culture.

Was the entertainment business beginning to take notice of you?
Absolutely not! In the '70s nobody in Hollywood gave a shit about documentaries. I just continued to make journalistic and cultural programs for KCET, and honed my skills. I was at KCET for seven and a half years. Finally I had to make a decision: either I pursued the course I was traveling and hopefully, it would lead me to becoming a producer for *60 Minutes* or a producer of network music specials, or I'd have to change directions completely and attempt to do what I'd secretly dreamed of all along: making narrative films. I never told anyone that I had this ambition, but I knew I had reached a crossroads. So I quit and starved for eight months, waiting for an opportunity to make a dramatic film.

Finally I found a L.A. social agency that wanted to do a short film on teenage pregnancy for public schools. Remembering how square the sex education films were when I was in school, I convinced them that I could make the most effective statement about this sensitive subject with a dramatic film.

I wrote, produced and directed *Teenage Father*, making it look like a documentary, but actually casting young actors in all the roles. The finished film was extremely effective when shown in classrooms. The kids believed it was real and were riveted to see young characters like themselves. However, when I showed it to adults, I hit trouble: These adults were also riveted, even moved emotionally, but when the credits came up at the end and they realized that this film was written and featured professional actors, they got angry, feeling that they'd been duped.

I realized that if I was going to submit *Teenage Father* to the Shorts Branch of the Academy, I'd have to do something drastic to alert a professional audience that this was not a documentary. This was the producer side of my brain working, not the director's side—so I shot a title card to go at the beginning of the film, saying: "The following film is fictional and features professional actors." This strategy worked, and my film won an Oscar for Best Dramatic Short Subject.

Surely that attracted industry attention.

Yes, that finally got me through the door. I signed with a brand new agency, CAA, which sent me around town to meet studio execs and producers. One of those CAA meetings was with the producers Gene Kirkwood and Howard Koch Jr. [now Hawk Koch], who had a project at United Artists called *The Idolmaker*. It was about the music world, which, of course, I was familiar with. They liked my ideas and convinced UA's David Field and Steve Bach to hire me to rewrite the script. There was no guarantee that the film would be made, but if it was, they said they'd let me direct.

That was really fast track, doing your own short film to directing a studio feature.

I knew what an opportunity this was, and I wasn't going to blow it. The film was set in the late '50s in New York City, and it was about Italian pop singers, having been adapted from the life of Bob Marcucci. Of course, I was a California kid, so I immediately buried myself in the New York City Italian ethos, studying every recent film about New York City Italians (like *Mean Streets*) and New York City street films like Fuller's *Pickup on South Street*. I wrote two drafts of the script over about two months, and amazingly, UA gave us the green light.

The Idolmaker got very good reviews, but did no business. One of our first screenings was at Radio City Music Hall, with 5,000 screaming teenagers—they loved it. Howard and Gene were jumping up and down saying: "We've got a hit." However, I was watching the people from United Artists, and they didn't look very happy—in fact, they looked glum. I asked why and one PR rep told me that *Heaven's Gate* had premiered in New York the night before. In fact, Steve Bach was on a plane at that very moment with [*Heaven's Gate* director Michael] Cimino and his cast, heading to Toronto to screen the film at the Festival. Except Steve was telling them that UA was cancelling the release, and the film was being postponed for re-editing.

Remember, at that point *Heaven's Gate* was the most expensive film of all time. The people from UA were seeing *doom*, and they didn't care about our little $3 million film. UA put *The Idolmaker* out for a couple of weeks, and got ready to close up shop.

Still, for me, it was a perfectly good situation. *The Idolmaker* got good reviews, and people in Hollywood saw the picture and liked it. In fact, Michael Eisner liked it enough to give me a deal at Paramount. The first project I developed at Paramount was a remake of *Out of the Past*, which I made later as *Against All Odds*. But while that script was being written, Don Simpson, the head of production, convinced me to direct a script that had been around for a long time, *An Officer and a Gentleman*.

Again you've made a huge leap, from a modestly budgeted feature to a big star vehicle.

No, remember that neither Richard Gere nor Debra Winger were stars until after *Officer*. But still, the budget was $7 million which was double *The Idolmaker* so, yes, it was a big jump for me.

While I had a great cast and a terrific crew helping me make *Officer*, the producer and Paramount made my life a nightmare during the shoot. Eisner had made me sign "a deal with the devil," agreeing to a schedule that was eight days less than his own VP of production had scheduled the picture. With all the bad weather in Washington State, I fell behind a day in the first two weeks. The producer didn't believe in the film, didn't believe in me and wanted to protect his ass with Paramount. So he tried to get me fired, and Don Simpson and Eisner bought into this plan. Only Richard Gere, Debra Winger and Lou Gossett stood behind me. With their help I was able to right the ship and get back on track.

Ultimately the film worked with the audience and was a big hit. Everyone knew that the producer had badmouthed his own picture, but he prospered anyway—like everyone else does when you have a hit. On the basis of that bad experience, I decided that I had to develop and produce my own movies.

Again, you have the capacity to make a career jump quickly, producing that fast.

I delivered a film to Paramount that grossed $125 million domestically, a huge success at that time, but Michael Eisner and Don Simpson immediately started playing games with me. Even though *Officer* had been the only film they'd made that year which made money, they weren't about to throw me a bone. They said, "We don't want to make *Against All Odds*, we want you to make *Flashdance* and *Footloose*." While I liked and respected Simpson, I realized that in order to prove myself as a producer I'd have to stay with the project I'd developed and see it through—that's producing. So Paramount put *Against All Odds* in turnaround. Now, I was really in the soup ... alone, with no studio. I asked Simpson not to announce to the town that Paramount had put my project in turnaround, and he agreed to do so for a month. Now, I had to prove that I was a producer. I had a line producer on board, a casting director, a designer, a location scout ... and they all agreed to work without pay to see if I could get the film set up.

For four weeks, we operated as if the film was happening, listing the production in the trades, taking meetings with actors, doing a location scout in Mexico. I financed what expenses we had out of my own pocket. My agent at CAA, Fred Specktor, called all the studios to see if he could stir up any interest. Finally Fred called and said that Guy McElwaine at Columbia loved *Officer*, and that he wanted to have lunch. So I had lunch with Guy, and I told him about *Against All Odds*. He immediately said, "I'll make it with you."

Guy McElwaine became my new "rabbi," and I desperately wanted to repay his confidence in me, but that wasn't easy. I loved Jeff Bridges for the role of Terry in *Against All Odds* but at that time, Jeff was dead in Hollywood because he had done *King Kong* for Dino de Laurentiis, which was not the blockbuster it had been touted to be. Still I told McElwaine that I wanted Jeff, and again he turned out to be a mensch: Guy said okay. By the way Frank Price, Columbia's chairman, concurred.

Jeff played a wide receiver, so I got Bob Chandler, who was an SC guy and played for the Raiders, to coach him. Again, as producer I was setting all this up ... finding trainers and nutritionists for Jeff, negotiating with the Raiders training camp to allow us to shoot at their facilities, negotiating with the Mexican government to allow us to shoot in their sacred Mayan ruins of Chichinitza and Tulu, which was the only American film ever to do so.

Out of the Past was a classic *film noir*, and most critics believe it to be one of the best of its genre. Unlike some filmmakers who follow the old blueprint closely, I didn't want my remake to be a copy of the old film, so the writer Eric Hughes and I changed the situation entirely. In effect, we designed a *film noir* to be shot in the sun—with the philosophy that the sun can be even more oppressive than shadow. We set our locations in Southern California and the Yucatan Mexico—Cancun, Isla Mujeres, Tulum and Chichen Itza, where the tropical sun can bore a hole through your head.

I was the sole creative producer of this film—developed the material, got the financing, worked with the writer and cast the stars. But I felt I needed a good line producer when the shooting began, so I hired Bill Gilmore. When we shot the famous race between Jake and Terry down the busiest part of Sunset Blvd. over two weekends, I needed to focus every ounce of my energy on being the director, so Bill Gilmore and Bill Borden, my associate producer-location manager, handled the huge logistical elements involved in this sequence.

After *The Idolmaker*, one thing I did realize was that market research was critical to a successful feature film. At that time, Joe Farrell was becoming a force in Hollywood. He had been a partner with Lou Harris, and was the first guy in the movie industry to deliver scientific, demographic market research. At first producers hated him, because he told them that there was no discernible audience for their film. But after he was proved right time and again, the studios all signed up with his company, NRG.

The first studio Joe Farrell contracted with was United Artists, and I immediately made friends with him. Joe had told my *Idolmaker* producers, Howard and Gene, "*The Idolmaker* is a bad title for this movie." He said the audience would be confused—that his research showed that most people thought it was a Biblical movie. They said, screw it, they'd keep the title. Well, they made a huge mistake, and very few people saw the film ... the title and marketing didn't work.

Right then on my first film, I learned from that experience how crucial good marketing was. I immediately had Fred Specktor negotiate into my new contract at Paramount that I had "consultation" on marketing. So that even though I wasn't a producer on *An Officer and a Gentleman*, I participated in the entire marketing of that film with Frank Mancuso and Gordon Weaver, the heads of Paramount Distribution & Marketing. They both became my mentors in those areas.

With *Against All Odds* at Columbia, I was the unquestioned producer and I made sure I was involved in marketing from the very beginning of the process: From changing the name of the movie (Marvin Antonowsky, head of marketing at Columbia, came up with the title *Against All Odds*) to creating a soundtrack for this film that had totally original songs that I could use in marketing.

Tell us about your use of music as a marketing tool.

With *Officer* I pioneered a new approach to music in dramatic films: "scorce"—actually, scoring dramatic scenes with popular records. Perhaps I wasn't the first director to do this, but I certainly brought this artistic technique to new heights. I probably used 15 songs under the action in *Officer*, but Paramount had given me no "source music" budget, only money for a score. My philosophy was that this film was about young, vibrant working-class people, and since in real life these people score their lives to contemporary music, why shouldn't my film characters do the same?

Again, I clashed with my producer and Paramount, namely Don Simpson and Michael Eisner. They said, "Take all those records out of the film." Luckily I disobeyed them and left those records in the soundtrack for the first test marketing screening. The audience absolutely loved the music. Since I had chosen album cuts that had not been hits, the actual cost was minimal. The entire soundtrack album cost under

$75,000. However, I didn't stop there. To end the film, I wanted an original title song that could be exploited as a major marketing tool for the film.

So I went to Joel Sill, president of music at Paramount, and told him that I wanted an original title song written and produced as a single record that could be marketed along with the film. Even though there was no money to record a title song in the budget, Joel began collaborating with me on a title song. Remember, I was not a producer on this film, but I was fulfilling a producer's function. Joel's brother Chuck Kaye, the head of A&M Publishing, suggested that one of his writers, Will Jennings, see the picture. I knew who Will Jennings was, because he'd recently collaborated with both Stevie Winwood and Eric Clapton on hit songs. That night I met Will Jennings and told him that I was looking for a title song for *Officer* that could be sung as a duet. He then saw the picture and returned the very next morning with a demo of the title song he'd written, "Up Where We Belong." He's written lyrics for two melodies featured in Jack Nitzsche's score. Joel and I immediately loved this demo and decided to get it recorded as a female and male duet.

As it turned out, my past in music came in handy, because I checked with two people I'd known in the music industry, Chris Blackwell of Island Records and Gary George, the former head of publicity at Warner Records, who had recently become a manager. Gary suggested his client, Jennifer Warnes, and Chris suggested Joe Cocker, who he had just signed to his label. Joel suggested his friend, Stuart Levine, to produce the record, and we moved forward. Meanwhile, Joel didn't tell anyone at Paramount that we were producing this title song.

The recording of "Up Where We Belong" was an epic story in itself. Stuart Levine first cut the track without the vocalists. Then Joe Cocker and Jennifer Warnes recorded their vocals at different times. The first time they actually sang together was on the Grammy Awards show. Finally we edited everything together with Bill Schnee, a great recording engineer, and the final version was absolute magic—or at least Joel and I thought so. When we played it for Michael Eisner and Don Simpson, they hated the record and said that it would never be a hit. They made me meet with various recording artist friends of theirs who tried to write songs, but their title songs didn't fit the movie. "Up

Where We Belong" had been written by Will Jennings using melodies from the film's score, so it fit perfectly.

Finally, Eisner and Simpson relented and the song went on the film. It turned out to be one of the biggest hits of the year—hitting the Top 10 the week that the film opened, and reaching #1 after three weeks. All that time, the record helped market the film—many times a day, radio disc jockeys would say, "This is from the film *An Officer and a Gentleman*," and all that promotion was free. Perhaps Eisner and Simpson didn't get it, but Frank Mancuso and Gordon Weaver definitely did.

But as I said, my life at Columbia was decidedly better than at Paramount. Guy McElwaine really did become my sponsor and gave me *carte blanche* to put together a source soundtrack of totally original songs for *Against All Odds*. At Columbia I met another studio VP of music, Gary LeMel. Like Joel Sill, he was a wonderful music-record man. Gary and I collaborated just as well as Joel and I had, and we put together not only a platinum soundtrack album (with major help from Doug Morris at Atlantic Records) but also another #1 title song by Phil Collins. Again, the music was a major promotional tool for marketing the film—every radio station played Phil's record dozens of times a day and the film reaped the benefits. After that, all producers wanted hit title songs from their films, but they found out it's harder than it looks.

There's a humorous note about getting Phil Collins to record *Against All Odds*. Phil was then the lead singer for Genesis, one of Atlantic's biggest acts. I first had to convince Phil's manager, Tony Smith, that recording the title song to my film would be a good career move for Phil's solo career. Then I had to meet with Phil and show him a rough cut of the film, which convinced him to take on the project. However, I then had to get an okay from Doug Morris, the president of Atlantic Records. Unfortunately, Doug did not like the idea, because Phil was currently touring and promoting a new Genesis album for Atlantic, and he thought that Phil having a single as a solo artist would detract from Genesis' album sales. When I met with him at his office in New York City, he flatly turned me down.

Dejected, I went to Kennedy to fly back to L.A., but my 6:30 American flight had been cancelled and I was put on the 7:30 flight. As I walked into the first class compartment, I couldn't believe my eyes,

There was Doug Morris sitting in seat 1-A. My seat was 3-A. I immediately asked the stewardess if I could sit with my "friend" in 1-B, and she agreed to change my seat. (I also tipped her $20.)

I went up and sat down next to Doug, saying, "Oh, what a coincidence." I then had six hours from New York to L.A to change his mind. By the time we landed, we were fast friends, and he gave his permission. Phil recorded a brilliant record and it went right to #1.

But even with that success, you hit an obstacle with the critics on **Against All Odds***: They liked the original better.*

Of course, they did. The original was a classic, and critics will always prefer the original classic over a remake. However, I didn't want to copy the director Jacques Tourneur's style, I wanted to do something different. At that time, critics could not get Robert Mitchum out of their minds. Jeff Bridges has proven himself to be a great actor, but at that time, the critics wouldn't accept him in Mitchum's original role. Although the film was successful, I will never do a remake again. You can't win.

However, we again broke new ground on that film. We shot in Mexico's sacred ruins, Chichen Itza and Tulum. No feature film, not even Mexican feature films, had ever been given permission to shoot there, nor has any feature film since. Using the ball court at Chichen was integral to my "*film noir* in the sun" concept, and I'm still very proud of those images. Certainly, conceiving the story in those locations was my creation as a director (along with Eric Hughes, the writer), but securing them was totally a produce-orial function, accomplished by Bill Gilmore and myself. I happen to speak fluent Spanish, which helps.

Your next film, **White Nights,** *was an unusual film for a studio to make.*

Again, this was another instance of a producer refusing to let a project die. That film was at three different studios, Orion, Paramount and Columbia, before it got made. I love dance, and I wanted to make an original dance movie where dance was intrinsic to the narrative, not a traditional "all singing, all dancing" film where plot and character stop once the dance sequences begin. I met with Mike Medavoy, head of production at Orion, and told him my concept. He liked my idea and introduced me to his friend Mikhail Baryshnikov, at the time the greatest ballet dancer in the world. I then suggested to Medavoy that we pair Baryshnikov with Gregory Hines, whose brilliant tap dancing I loved. Mike agreed, and I began interviewing writers about a concept. This was not an easy task, pairing two dancers of different nationalities, different races and different dance styles. James Goldman of *Lion in Winter* came up with the "Russian defector" concept, and I loved it.

Your political newsman background was perfect for that kind of story.

Yes, I was terribly excited, because this was an opportunity to combine art and politics into a new genre—an international political-dance thriller. However, Mike Medavoy's bosses at Orion were not so excited by this concept. Eric Plescow and Arthur Krimm said, "No way." So Mike had to put the project in turnaround. I set it up at Paramount under my deal there, but again, Simpson and Eisner refused to make it, putting it in turnaround. Again, Guy McElwaine came to my rescue. It's great when you have the head of a studio believe in you, and I owe a huge amount to Guy for believing.

White Nights was a true international production. We shot in England, Scotland, Portugal and Finland for Russia. Actually, we even shot in Russia, using a Finnish film crew who secretly shot footage of Leningrad. Of course, when the film was released, most film critics were oblivious, saying, "Yet again, Helsinki doubles for Russia." As I said before, you can't win.

In post-production, my music supervisor Phil Ramone and I came up with several other original songs which I used to score the action of the film, reaffirming the contemporary nature of the material. Artists like Robert Plant, Lou Reed, John Hyatt, Roberta Flack, Nile Rogers, and Chaka Khan and Mike Rutherford contributed excellent records to the soundtrack.

You had two #1s from this film.

Yes, I put together two original title songs for *White Nights*, "Separate Lives" by Phil Collins and Marilyn Martin and "Say You, Say Me" by Lionel Ritchie. Neither record had the name of the film in its title, but it didn't matter—they both promoted the film brilliantly, and they both become #1 records. They were both nominated for an Academy Award, with "Say You, Say Me" winning the Oscar.

Again, what I was doing was using music to position this very unique genre of a dance film in the contemporary marketplace. *White Nights* is a difficult concept to sell—a Russian ballet dancer and an American tap dancer, both defectors, collaborate and use their talents to escape the Soviet Union. Doesn't sound very commercial, does it? But when audiences hear Lionel Ritchie singing "Say You, Say Me" on the radio, and the disc jockey says, "From the movie *White Nights* which I saw last night, and it has records from all these great contemporary artists, go see it," it definitely clues a young audience that there's something for them in this film.

You had the idea for La Bamba *way back when you started out at KCET.*

At KCET I became very good friends with Danny Valdez, a wonderful Chicano singer. His brother Luis Valdez was an important political force in the Chicano Movement, having worked closely with Cesar Chavez on the grape strike.

One night Danny and I were having a beer, and he suggested that we make a film about Ritchie Valens, the only artist to have a #1 record on the American charts in Spanish, "La Bamba." Danny was good-looking and a dynamic singer, so of course he wanted to play Ritchie, but neither of us had 35 cents to our names. So for the time being, that idea stayed a dream.

However, once I started having success in Hollywood, Danny called me up. He said, "What about *La Bamba*?" I said, "Great idea," and Guy let me develop it at Columbia. I asked Luis to write the script and he did a wonderful job, but this project was not on the "fast track" at Columbia.

I saw a major opportunity for this film to break new ground in Hollywood. Remember, I had served in the Peace Corps in [Bolivia], and after I returned I started to realize that the American Southwest was going through a sea change. Since I spoke fluent Spanish, I heard all around me a huge Latino groundswell, an immigrant population that had become *the* labor force in Southern California. So I went to Guy and said: "You guys are really missing the boat." He immediately perked up and asked why. I told him that Columbia was trying to capture the largest audience possible for its films, but they were totally missing the fastest growing segment of the population: Latinos.

At that time, Columbia Pictures was owned by Coca-Cola, and I reminded him that Coke was one of the few companies that truly understood how to market to the Latino population. He was intrigued and immediately put *La Bamba* on the fast track for production. I told him that I'd produce, but I wanted Luis Valdez to direct this film, sending a message to the Latino community that the first Hollywood film about a major Chicano artist would be written and directed by a Chicano. Again, Guy supported me, so Luis Valdez became the director of *La Bamba*. He did a fantastic job, and our film is still the most successful Latino-themed film ever to come out of Hollywood.

Our concept for *La Bamba* was simple: To make a film that fits into that long ethos of Hollywood immigrant movies. We cast our movie with Lou Diamond Philips, Esai Morales, Rosanna DeSoto and Elizabeth Peña—great Latino actors who embodied the '50s immigrant experience in California.

Again, *La Bamba* had a major musical quotient, and I knew the perfect group to re-record Ritchie's music: Los Lobos. They were great musicians from East Los Angeles, and were just breaking as a hot alternative rock band. They understood how to keep Ritchie's raw energy and put just enough modern spin on our records to make them contemporary. It worked, and for the second time *La Bamba* went right to #1 on the pop charts. We released the film simultaneously in English and Spanish versions, the first Hollywood film to do so. The response was amazing. *La Bamba* did 18 percent of its business in Spanish. I expected it to play well in the United States. What I didn't expect was that it would also play well internationally. The film ran for a year in Paris and made a lot of money for Columbia across Europe.

In some ways you function as a lawyer because you must convince people to do things that they don't want to do.
That's what producers do. Sometimes a producer conceives a project. Sometimes a director has the vision. But it's a producer's function

to sell that vision and pull everything together to maximize that vision. You've got to sell the writer on a concept, you've got to sell the studio to finance the script, and you've constantly got to act as cheerleader to convince everyone to believe in the project.

I learned from *The Idolmaker* and *An Officer*, two films I didn't produce, how important it was to control the entire process. The success of *Officer* gave me a chance to produce, and since then I've been pushing these projects up steep hills toward production. In every instance the reaction is similar: No one believes but me. Sometimes my films get made and sometimes they don't, but you can't stop pushing and believing in them, or nothing will get made. It was the same with *Against All Odds*, *White Nights*, *La Bamba* ... all seemingly non-commercial films which all made money.

After La Bamba *you moved studios to Warner Bros. Why?*

Guy McElwaine had left Columbia and although his successor, David Puttnam, did a terrific job of marketing *La Bamba*, I thought I'd try my luck at Warners, which was a very successful studio. They wanted me to make music films, but before I could develop anything, they suggested I make *Everybody's All-American*. This was the first script I had not developed in a long time, but I loved it. Tom Rickman adapted Frank Deford's novel brilliantly. When I read the script, I was hooked. The subject was SEC football in the 1950s, with all these tragic Southern characters—they just jumped off the page.

Everybody's All-American is about the last great white running back in the '50s, but it's also an epic tale about the South and how it changed from the '50s to the '70s. What also intrigued me was the opportunity to examine America's obsession with success—the adulation, even *worship* it pours on its heroes, until they can no longer perform—then casts them aside like old newspapers. The logistical issues were immense. Americans are experts at football and watch a vast number of college and professional games every weekend, so our football sequences had to be authentic.

The first thing I did was call Steve Sabol of NFL Films, the repository of great footage from NFL games throughout history. I needed NFL Films to collaborate with me in building the professional football sequences. Happily, Steve was a very classy gentleman, and he agreed to give me access to his library. I then hired a professional football coach, Lew Erber, to recruit a group of ex-professional and ex-collegiate players who would be our "professional" extras in the film.

I'd already scouted most of the major SEC universities, and finally settled on LSU, because of its fantastic football tradition. Tiger Stadium, or "Death Valley" as it's called by visiting teams, was built by Huey Long in the '30s, and it's awesome. We approached the football sequences almost like another film—shooting with a second unit for two weeks prior to the beginning of principal photography. Through Steve Sabol's NFL Films, we'd found some wonderful footage of a running back-wide receiver whose career had taken him from the Washington Redskins to the Denver Broncos. This became our template for Gavin Grey's professional career.

By the way, while the design of how we shot the football sequences was a directorial function, the liaising with the university's adminis-tration and securing permission was definitely produce-orial. We were able to shoot all of our college football sequences inside Tiger Stadium with 90,000 LSU fans looking on. Dennis and our players had rehearsed each play like a performance. I had my camera positions all mapped out. So, ten minutes before the game, when the stands were full, we ran our plays with military precision. Then at halftime, we ran another series of plays during the seven minutes we were allotted. The resulting shots of Dennis Quaid and his LSU teammates winning the 1959 National Championship in front of 90,000 screaming fans was electrifying.

Everybody's All-American was meant to be an American tragedy, which was what interested me, but American audiences don't like to see their heroes fall from grace, so the film was not the box-office suc-cess that Warner Bros. had hoped it would be.

It's like that Springsteen song, "Glory Days."

Yes, the tragedy in *Everybody's All-American* is what gives it pro-fundity and depth, but the movie business is about making money at the box office, and this was my first box office failure. Certain people in Hollywood love to see others fail, and after five moneymaking films, I got a taste of that Hollywood *invidia*—a Spanish word for celebrating others' failures.

At this point you set up you own company, New Visions Inc.

I'd been building this production company at two different studios, and I'd recruited a loyal group of people to work with me. Since I'd always told them that I wanted to build something independent, a company that could produce, finance and distribute its own pictures, they started to believe me and then to put on the pressure to deliver on my ambitious plan. *La Bamba* was a template for my concept of producing low-budget films, and hadn't it worked brilliantly? They thought that this was the time to strike, and they pointed out that many industry people had started to take notice.

My advisors at the time were against it: My agents at CAA, Fred Specktor and Mike Ovitz, and Warner execs Bob Daly and Terry Semel, all said: "That's not what you do.... You're a filmmaker ... make films and let the professionals distribute them." Looking back, I wish that I'd listened to them, but since I'd indoctrinated my employees with the dream of building an independent studio, I had to follow through. The allure of owning my own shop was just too great.

Producing and directing is very consuming, but running a studio is jumping into a much bigger swimming pool. You're not only developing material and then deciding which films to make, overseeing production and post-production, but also you're designing the marketing and distribution of those films. It's a huge whirlpool that never stops.

New Visions made seven films before we went bust. What I realized from this experience was that Specktor, Ovitz, Daly and Semel had been right: Being an executive had been a misuse of my talent. Yes, I enjoyed running my little studio, but since I wasn't creatively on-the-line, risking everything on my own talent, I was not really fulfilled. Yes, the failure of New Visions was painful, but it gave me the opportunity to return to what I truly love, filmmaking.

Your next project was a real departure for you, Blood In, Blood Out.

Yes, it was a Chicano gangster picture that I'd developed at New Visions. When New Visions imploded, I decided to make *Blood In, Blood Out* myself. What was unusual was the studio that wanted to partner with me on this picture—Disney. When I was at Paramount,

Jeff Katzenberg has been a junior executive under Don Simpson and Michael Eisner. I had always gotten along with Jeff, who was smart and an incredibly hard worker. He had moved to Disney with Eisner and was head of production. When he heard that I wanted to make a Latin-based project, he immediately showed interest. Even when he found out that my project was going to be an epic Chicano gangster picture, he didn't shy away and made the deal.

Like I'd convinced Guy McElwaine about *La Bamba*, I sold Jeff on the premise that the Latino audience was becoming huge, and like all American immigrant groups, Latinos had to start at the bottom of the economic ladder. I hired a first-time screenwriter, the great Chicano poet Jimmy Santiago Baca, who gave my project both Latino cred and amazingly authentic scenes and dialogue—Jimmy had spent eight years in a federal penitentiary in New Mexico before turning his life around and winning the National Book Award for poetry.

I'm extremely proud of this production, because the film was bilingual and introduced a cast of talented unknown Chicano actors who have gone on to successful careers: Ben Bratt, Jesse Borrego, Damian Chapa, Enrique Castillo, Danny Trejo, Raymond Cruz and Valente Rodriguez. We also gave lifts to the careers of Billy Bob Thornton, Ving Rhames, Delroy Lindo and Tom Tolls.

I wanted total authenticity in the making of this picture, so I had to convince the California prison system to allow us to shoot in San Quentin, where the story originally took place. The process of securing one of the most famous prisons in America, a heavy duty joint, was totally a produce-orial function. Daniel Vasquez, the warden, was a tough nut, but he finally agreed. I thought of *Blood In, Blood Out* as my opportunity to make a hard-edged prison genre film in the tradition of *White Heat* or *I Am a Fugitive from a Chain Gang*, except that this was the true-life story of the birth of the Mexican Mafia, the most powerful modern crime family in America.

Disney had been very supportive during the making of *Blood In*, but during post-production in the summer of 1992, all hell broke loose—the L.A. riots! After the riots, Michael Eisner, the chairman of Disney, asked to see the film and freaked. He said he wasn't about to risk releasing a film that might cause a public incident. Katzenberg pled our case to Frank Wells, who was co-chairman of Disney with Eisner, the only person he would listen to. Fortunately, Wells liked the film and weighed in in our favor.

Still, Eisner handled the film with kid gloves. He asked his head of marketing, Bob Levin, to test the film around the country to see what the reaction was. We tested in Sacramento, Oakland, Rochester, El Paso, New York City and Las Vegas. These screenings actually encouraged Levin, who predicted that the film would gross $40 million at the box office in the U.S. However, when a fistfight broke out in the lobby of a Las Vegas cinema, the last test site, Eisner used that incident to kill any wide release. *Blood In, Blood Out* had its name changed to *Bound by Honor* and was given a small, obscure release. The results at the box office were predictable ... meager. However, its salvation came in its home video release.

How do you have the emotional resilience to deal with that kind of thing?

You just have to survive it. This town changes its attitude toward you and puts your career in cold storage—"Siberia." During my time in "Siberia," I read a script that had been developed from a Stephen King novel at Castle Rock: *Dolores Claiborne*. The writer, Tony Gilroy, had done a fabulous adaptation, and I went after the project. I got on well with Martin Shafer, the head of production at Castle Rock, and he gave me the gig. I then worked with Tony on the script and we took it through two more drafts before Martin gave us a green light.

Dolores was a psychological thriller, something I had never done before, which suited me just fine. Most of my films have no relationship to one another other, except that all my films are about working class characters. I think of filmmaking as a journey, and I don't like to travel the same road twice.

Dolores is a definitely woman's movie. The three main characters are strong, difficult women, and we chose two fabulous actresses to collaborate with Kathy Bates: Jennifer Jason Leigh and Judy Parfitt. Stylistically, it was a giant step forward for me, because the story is told in flashbacks, jumping from the present, to 25 years before. That was Tony Gilroy's brilliant idea. Two stories took place simultaneously 25 years apart. I'm extremely proud of the visual style of this film, and the fact that women have warmly embraced it.

Larry Kasdan told me that his son attended a class at Columbia film school where his teacher showed my film, saying: "Only a woman director could have made *Dolores Claiborne*." Larry's son raised his hand and said, "I think Taylor Hackford is a man." And the teacher said, "No, she's definitely a woman." [*Laughs*] That was a great compliment to me.

Is your producer side ever at odds with your director side?

All the time, but as I said earlier, the reason I became a producer was to protect myself as a director. My producing focus is development, pre- and post-production and marketing. When I'm actually shooting, I always cede my producing power to a line producer, so I can focus on the truly creative part of filmmaking. While I want a collaborator who will support me in capturing my vision, I also need someone who will argue with me about practical logistics. You wouldn't be interviewing me now if I wasn't foremost a director but I would never have made as many films, if hadn't done my job as a producer to get them financed, produced and marketed.

A good example of a film developed from scratch is *Proof of Life*, with Russell Crowe and Meg Ryan, which was also written by Tony Gilroy. We took an article from *Vanity Fair* about kidnap and ransom and developed it with Castle Rock. It was a very arduous production. We shot around the world on three continents, using crew from 20 different countries, who spoke 13 different languages. When you are shooting a movie that challenging, you aren't always checking on what's happening off the set, and during *Proof*, Russell Crowe and Meg Ryan had an affair. Inevitably, the media found out, and it became a major news item because Meg had a husband and child. The resulting scandal definitely hurt our film.

At a press conference in Europe a reporter cornered me and asked, "This big affair must have helped your film." While I'm usually very cool in handling the press, I responded honestly: "No, it actually hurt it." Russell Crowe never forgave me for this remark and has been openly hostile ever since. The rule is: A producer should always bite his or her tongue and not discuss the cast's personal life. I spoke the truth about a circumstance that had compromised my film. I shouldn't have.

So I've had two instances when real events sabotaged my movies.

The release of *Blood In, Blood Out* was compromised by the L.A. riots, and the release of *Proof of Life* was overshadowed by a huge media story about the stars of the film having an affair. In both cases, there was nothing I could do about it.

What about Ray? Was that percolating all this time?

I secured the rights to *Ray* at New Visions, but after my company folded, I couldn't get anyone to finance the development of a script. I sat down and wrote a treatment for the film in the early '90s, but still no studio would step up. They'd say, "Nobody cares about Ray Charles. He is passé. He's an old man. Nobody listens to that music any more." They continued saying that for 11 years but, thankfully, Ray didn't take the rights away from me. Finally Stuart Benjamin, as my ex-partner from New Visions, went to work for billionaire Phil Anschutz at Crusader Entertainment. Phil is really a very interesting guy, a tough businessman who had very conservative political and religious beliefs. However, he loved Ray Charles and agreed to develop a script.

We hired a black writer, Jimmy White, to adapt my treatment into the *Ray* screenplay. It was epic, covering 40 years in the life of this incredible man. However, even when Phil Anschutz promised to 50 percent of the budget and 50 percent of the marketing, no studio would step up. We went back to the drawing board and brought on another writer, Bob Eisley, who did some terrific work on the script, bringing it down in size. Finally, Anschutz decided that he'd finance the film personally, an incredible decision for which I will always be grateful to him.

He committed $30 million to make the film, but since the film was period and still covered 40 years in Ray Charles' life, it was going to be a real stretch to make it. However, New Mexico and Louisiana had just passed tax incentive laws to encourage productions to come shoot in their states. By coincidence, I had been partially responsible for conceiving the Louisiana plan, so it was amazing that my advisory work for Louisiana's new tax incentive program actually made it possible for me to make my dream project, *Ray*.

New Orleans doubled for ten other U.S. cities, but few people ever knew it when they saw the film on the screen. After it was shot and edited, we again made the rounds of every studio as he had with the script, showing them the finished film. Again, they all turned us down, except one studio: Universal. As it turned out, Ron Meyer, the chairman of Universal, had snuck into a Ray Charles concert at the Hollywood Palladium when he was 13 years old and had never forgotten the experience. He loved the film and agreed to have Universal distribute it worldwide.

The rest of this story is very positive. *Ray* premiered at the Toronto Film Festival, receiving very strong reviews. It opened in the U.S. to $20 million and ultimately grossed $75 million domestic. The film received six Academy Award nominations. Likewise, the international sales were extremely gratifying. To date the film has grossed over $500 million worldwide.

With all the success that Ray *had, things must have gotten easier for you in getting projects off the ground.*

Not really. Yes, I got some offers to do certain films that didn't appeal to me. It's been my career curse that I can only pursue projects I have a passion for, and often no one wants to make those projects. After *Ray*, I set my sights on making a film about Julia Butterfly Hill, the environmental activist who lived alone for two years at the top of Luna, a huge redwood tree in Humbolt County. She lived 20 stories high, up in the branches of this ancient redwood, protecting it from being cut down. A conglomerate that owned most of the great redwood forest around Luna tried everything it could to remove her: Setting up a blockade to starve her out, flashing bright lights and playing loud music 24 hours a day to drive her crazy. They even tried to blow her out of Luna with a Chinook helicopter. She persevered and ultimately brought corporate America to its knees.

This was an incredible woman's story, and since four out of the six Hollywood studios were then being run by women, I thought it was a natural. It wasn't. It was *Ray* all over again, nobody wanted to make it. Some actresses understood the potential of *Luna*—I convinced Anne Hathaway to play the title role—but still no one would finance it.

It was a tragedy because I knew this film could have been a commercial hit. It was full of action, jeopardy and drama. I spent a year and a half trying to get *Luna* made, but it just wasn't going to happen.

At that point my agent asked me to meet a man who was starting a small studio. His name was David Bergstein and his company was Capitol Films. David said that he'd love to make a film with me, although *Luna* was not to his taste. My wife, Helen Mirren, had just won the Oscar for *The Queen*, so she had some Hollywood heat.

A friend, Mark Jacobson, a staff writer for *New York* magazine, had written a script called *Love Ranch*, which was a *roman à clef* about a murder at the infamous Mustang Ranch in Reno, Nevada. The story focused on a love triangle featuring brothel owner, Joe Comforte, his wife Sally and a world heavyweight boxing contender, Oscar Bonavena, who had fought Muhammad Ali.

It was an opportunity to work with my wife, and Bergstein liked the idea. I then met with Joe Pesci, who I thought would be perfect to play Comforte. Pesci liked the idea of working with Helen and signed on. Mark Jacobson sent me a tape of a young Spanish actor, Sergio Peris-Mencheta, who was big and handsome like Bonavena. He came to Los Angeles to audition with Helen, and we both agreed that he'd be terrific to fill out our cast.

Capitol Films set our budget at $16 million, but they said that we could apply any rebate we received to augment the budget. New Mexico had pioneered film incentives along with Louisiana, and I had gone there several years before to speak at a convention of film commissioners from around the country. Governor Bill Richardson and his New Mexico Film Commission were very welcoming to us, and we committed to shoot in and around Albuquerque, which was a perfect match for Reno, Nevada.

From the beginning of production we had problems with Capitol Films. My co-producer Marty Katz and I struggled every week to get enough money from Capitol to make our payroll. The frustration was palpable—I was trying to motivate my crew and get performances from my cast, while all the time knowing that we might not be able to pay them on Friday. Twice during principal photography we actually didn't make payroll, but we convinced the crew to come back the following week by offering to pay them a premium of 25 percent. To everyone's surprise, Bergstein actually paid the extra 25 percent. We finally made it through principal photography, but then the "no money" scenario started all over again in post-production. Instead of a 17-week finishing schedule for *Love Ranch*, we spent over one year finishing the film. By the time it came out, 18 months later, there had been such bad publicity that the critics and the public hardly took notice. Still, I stayed through the process and got the film finished. Making independent films can be very precarious, and the experience of *Love Ranch* had been a textbook example of what can go wrong. However, I did get to work with Helen and that experience was wonderful.

As I've said before, you just have to get up, dust yourself off and jump back into the fray. My agent got a call from foreign sales agent Nick Meyer at Sierra Affinity Films, who was interested in meeting me for a crime genre film they were going to make with action star Jason Statham. Jason was to play a famous literary character, Parker, from the series of books by Richard Stark [the *nom de plume* of Donald Westlake]. I am a big fan of the Parker books, so this proposition was of real interest to me. Although Jason is English and Parker is American, I thought that Statham's strong, silent and dangerous persona would be perfect for this character. I met Jason, we hit it off and decided to work together.

Nick Meyer then sold domestic rights to Peter Schlessel's Film District, a new independent company that had had some recent box office successes. Peter wanted a female star for *Parker* who would put some heat into the equation with Jason. I suggested Jennifer Lopez, with whom I had developed an early project, which never got made. Peter agreed that Jennifer would be great. I described the part of Leslie to her, and specifically said that I wanted a 'messy divorcee, pushing 40, whose life had turned out all wrong.' I wanted this character to be vulnerable, but at the same time tough enough to go for a final lunge at "the ring." Without hesitating, Jennifer agreed to play the part.

We again shot in New Orleans, but I found that the tax incentive that I'd helped originate had changed the Crescent City into a dynamic production center. There were many excellent crews available and several more stages had been built since I had been there eight years before.

Like every film, there were logistical nightmares on *Parker*, but ours started even before we began to shoot. We had a very tight budget, so we wanted to shoot as much of the film as possible in New Orleans to take advantage of Louisiana's wonderful rebate. Therefore, even though the story begins with a heist at the Ohio State Fair, the biggest state fair in the country, we planned to shoot those heist sequences at a small Baton Rouge amusement park, and then intercut this "dramatic footage" with wide views of the Ohio State Fair shot by a second unit.

Frankly, this decision was a major compromise, because we would only have about 700 extras in Baton Rouge, while there are between 50,000 and 75,000 people a day at the Ohio State Fair. Still, we could not afford to take our entire crew and cast to Ohio, so I worked out a design I hoped would allow these two different locations to fit together seamlessly.

Then with only four days left before we were supposed to start shooting, disaster hit. The owner of the Baton Rouge amusement park reneged on our deal and demanded three times the fee we had negotiated. He thought he could hold up these big, rich Hollywood people. In reality, we didn't have any extra money. So when something like this happens, what does a producer do? You improvise. My line producer Stratton Leopold and I called the people at the Ohio State Fair and told them about our plight. I then asked them if we could bring Jason, our other actors and a small, mobile crew to Ohio and shoot our principal photography while the fair was actually going on. Effectively, we would not be controlling what was going on, but spontaneously "grabbing our sequences" as tens of thousands of patrons were enjoying the Fair. Unbelievably, the people at the Ohio State Fair agreed, and within three days we mobilized our cast and crew and flew to Columbus, Ohio. We got production value we could never have dreamed of in Baton Rouge— literally 50,000 extras surrounding our actors. It gave the film a huge opening sequence.

Our shooting in New Orleans went smoothly, and then we moved to Palm Beach to capture the finale of the film. The novelist had made Palm Beach a "hero" location for the climax heist at the end of the novel, and anyone who knows Palm Beach knows that it's configured like an impregnable island—with its billionaires living inside the best security system in the United States. Since Palm Beach is incredibly beautiful, I was more than happy to use it as the set-piece for the climax. What I didn't know was that those same Palm Beach billionaires have no interest in the media seeing inside their little haven. In fact, the city government had passed an ordinance that prevented any film or TV show from shooting inside the municipality.

I set about trying to convince the Palm Beach City Council to allow us to shoot in Palm Beach proper. Ultimately the city attorney dug in his heals, and intimidated the council into voting down our "special, one-time permit" allowing us to shoot in Palm Beach. Now, this may sound like a total failure, but in reality it was a major coup for us because it brought our plight to the attention of the citizens of Palm Beach, many of whom were sympathetic to our cause. The local press was also sympathetic, and even the fire and police chiefs expressed regret that the council had voted us down.

With all this unofficial good will, Palm Beach Country Film Commissioner Chuck Eldard quietly pointed out to me that the City Council didn't actually control the main thoroughfares on the island, including the four bridges connecting Palm Beach to the mainland—they belonged to the state and county, and he controlled them. So we were able to shoot with Jason and Jennifer on all of these major, recognizable thoroughfares, proving that the film was shot in Palm Beach.

If that wasn't enough, Chuck Eldard mobilized his county and state contacts to shut down all four bridges connecting Palm Beach to the mainland. All the drawbridges were opened simultaneously, police helicopters slashed through the night sky, and police patrol boats cut through Worth Lake with their searchlights flashing. It was the spectacular sequence I needed at the end of the film.

This complete shut-down of all access to Palm Beach lasted for 35 minutes during magic hour, and the City of Palm Beach did absolutely nothing to stop us. Why? I believe it was because as producers we had been courteous and respectful of the City Council's process, and had not badmouthed them in the media for turning us down. Ultimately, they turned a blind eye and let us shoot.

So what's next?

Whatever it is, I know it won't be easy. I never stop developing projects, but it's getting more and more difficult every year to get projects financed, because the industry's business model has changed. Because of digital piracy, studios no longer have the luxury of time in releasing feature films. They know that the moment a film is released in a cinema, it will be copied and stolen by pirates who will immediately upload it to the Internet where it will be offered in file-sharing networks or in digital lockers, ostensibly "for free." This shock to our traditional system of distribution has caused studios to alter the nature of the films they are making. They want films that can be mass-marketed around the world on the same weekend.

Of course, any film that needs "special" handling or a "gradual release" to allow the audience to discover it, doesn't fit into this new "make-it-quick" scenario. So these types of films, the kinds of films I've made during my career, are not being produced. Or if they are being made, their budgets are being squeezed so mercilessly that production values and visual sophistication suffers ... meaning quality goes down.

I'm not saying that the current digital piracy crisis can't be addressed and effectively solved, but it's going to take a major consensus among the talented people in our industry—artists in front of and behind the camera, executives and Teamsters, local and state politicians and software and hardware manufacturers. We must educate young people, who have been weaned on the Internet, not to expect everything to be free—that paying for intellectual property is vital to preserving their own culture and identity. Artists create, and their creations make our culture grow and prosper. But what happens if we artists are not able to prosper from the work we create? We've got to be able to pay our rent from what we create. Otherwise, we'll choose to do something else. It's simple: Every producer is trying to create something that will reach an audience and, in doing so, make them and their collaborators a living.

HACKFORD'S FILMOGRAPHY

Producer
Parker (2013)
Love Ranch (2010)
Ray (2004)
Proof of Life (2000)
G:MT Greenwich Mean Time (1999)
When We Were Kings (documentary, 1996)
Dolores Claiborne (1995)
Blood In, Blood Out (1993)

Everybody's All-American (1988)
La Bamba (1987)
White Nights (1985)
Against All Odds (1984)
Bukowski (documentary, 1973)

Executive Producer
A Place to Stand (documentary, 2014)
The Devil's Advocate (1997)
Defenseless (1991)

Sweet Talker (1991)
Mortal Thoughts (1991)
Queens Logic (1991)
The Long Walk Home (1990)
Rooftops (1989)

Director
Parker (2013)
Love Ranch (2010)
Ray (2004)
Proof of Life (2000)
The Devil's Advocate (1997)
When We Were Kings (documentary, 1996)

Dolores Claiborne (1995)
Blood In, Blood Out (1993)
Everybody's All-American (1988)
La Bamba (1987)
Chuck Berry Hail! Hail! Rock'n'Roll (documentary, 1987)
White Nights (1985)
Against All Odds (1984)
An Officer and a Gentleman (1982)
The Idolmaker (1980)

Mark Johnson

Mark Johnson won the Academy Award for Best Picture for Rain Man, directed by Barry Levinson, and starring Dustin Hoffman and Tom Cruise.

Johnson produced all of writer-director Barry Levinson's films from 1982 to 1994. In addition to Rain Man, their eclectic slate of films included The Natural, Tin Men, Toys, Young Sherlock Holmes, Avalon, Diner, Good Morning, Vietnam and Bugsy, which was nominated for ten Academy Awards, including Best Picture and Best Director. Bugsy won a Best Picture Golden Globe.

Johnson and Levinson's 1994 break-up was amicable. Johnson established his own production company; his maiden film, A Little Princess (1995), won the Los Angeles Film Critics New Generation Award for director Alfonso Cuaron. Johnson quickly followed up with two very different films, the down-home Southern comedy Home Fries and the mob thriller Donnie Brasco. Those early efforts augured Johnson's future assorted slate of productions, including TV fare. During the period, he served as executive producer for L.A. Doctors and Falcone and also executive-produced The Guardian. More recently, he executive-produced the groundbreaking hit series Breaking Bad.

An affable and engaging personality, Johnson has produced films for virtually every studio, including, as examples: My Dog Skip (Warner Bros.), Galaxy Quest (DreamWorks), The Notebook (New Line) and the Chronicles of Narnia franchise (Buena Vista). His financially successful mainstream films enable him to indulge his passion for making smaller independent pictures with new talent, such as Ballast, which won acclaim at the 2008 Sundance Film Festival. Johnson's production company, Gran Via, holds a first-look pact to produce family films for Walden.

Johnson produces films both big and small. His films encompass a wide array of genres and a wide reservoir of talent, including: Nick Cas-

savetes' drama My Sister's Keeper; The Notebook, *based on Nicholas Sparks' best-selling novel; the sci-fi spoof* Galaxy Quest, *directed by Dean Parisot;* The Rookie *directed by John Lee Hancock; Clint Eastwood's* A Perfect World, *starring Kevin Costner, and the children's book* How to Eat Fried Worms.

Johnson's recent motion pictures are, characteristically, not easily categorized. They include the Chronicles of Narnia *movies as well as the low-budget horror film* Don't Be Afraid of the Dark. *With a taste for '60s rock 'n' roll, Johnson produced* Not Fade Away, *written and directed by David Chase.*

For the Sundance Channel, Johnson executive-produced the dramatic series Rectify, *written by Ray McKinnon.* Rectify *revolves around a man, released from Death Row based on DNA evidence, struggling to rebuild his life because some still think he's guilty.*

Johnson served as chairman of the Academy of Motion Picture Arts and Sciences' Foreign Language Film award selection committee and is a member of the Board of Governors of the Academy (Producers Branch).

A graduate of the University of Virginia, Johnson earned an M.A.

Mark Johnson, 2013. Courtesy Mark Johnson.

in Film Scholarship from the University of Iowa. His grad-school room-mate was future film author and educator David Bordwell. After grad-uating, Johnson departed Iowa City for New York, where he entered the Directors Guild Training Program.

Johnson first worked as a director trainee on Paul Mazursky's Next Stop, Greenwich Village. *He subsequently relocated to Los Angeles and moved up to assistant director on* Movie, Movie, The Brink's Job, Escape from Alcatraz *and Mel Brooks'* High Anxiety, *where he formed a friend-ship and professional relationship with one of the film's writers, Barry Levinson.*

Duane Byrge: You said something very interesting at the Vir-ginia Film Festival. You said that your best producing was getting Diner *to Pauline Kael, film critic for* The New Yorker.

Mark Johnson: I was an executive producer, working for Jerry Weintraub, who was the producer. Even though it was the first film I was ever involved with, I realized early on that we were in trouble because MGM really didn't like the movie. They wanted it to be more like *Porky's*, one of those screw-around movies where guys are trying to get drunk and laid. That wasn't what it was. We were convinced that it was a really good movie.

It turns out that Pauline Kael was a good friend of my mother's. So I asked her if she'd see the movie. I snuck it off to her. We showed it to her and James Wolcott the writer. She saw it and loved it. She called MGM and basically said, "You guys are going to have egg on your face because in two weeks I'm going to write a rave review, and the movie is not going to be out."

She sort of shamed them into opening it in one theater in Man-hattan. It's really thanks to Pauline that the movie saw the light of day and got the kind of attention that it did. I grew up reading Pauline Kael. She was one of the few critics, even if I disagreed with her, I loved to read her. Just the fact that she was seeing a film that I was involved with was a big thrill for me. When she was alive, I showed her every movie that I produced, and she didn't like any of them. Actually, she did like *Bugsy*. She was a huge Jim Toback fan.

Producing is so many different things. It's the beauty of producing that there really isn't a guidebook. There is no one way to do it, and every producer works differently. There are some very good producers who are not directly involved in the making of a film, but they're very good at protecting a film. Their strength may be in helping to market it, or keeping the filmmaker protected from the studio, or from whoever is financing it.

The area that I most need help in is delegating, even though I have really good people around me. I have Tom Williams, who develops and has been the executive producer on several of our movies now. He runs our film division—or, rather, he *is* our film division. I don't want it to sound like we have a whole division—he is the guy. We have Melissa Bernstein, who runs TV and co-executive produce[d] *Breaking Bad*. Also we have Mark Chiriac, who reports to both of them. That is it.

It's very hard these days to finish a call. We have so much going on. There's always some emergency. I love what I'm doing, but I think I could be more productive if I let things go. The thing is that studios and directors, filmmakers want you when they want you. They don't want to hear, "I'm in Wisconsin now on another movie and I'll get back to you as soon as I can." One of the tricks I learned early on is that you never talk to a director or a studio executive who you are working on one movie about any of the other movies you're working on. You want them to believe that this is the only thing you're working on, even if they know it is not true.

You're still like a kid in the candy store when it comes to what you're doing.

I'm the luckiest person that I know because I'm doing what I've always wanted to do. As a kid I never thought in a thousand years that I'd get to do it. I am as excited today as when I started. A lot of my contemporaries are not. They don't particularly like the business as it is now. My feeling is that it's different, but it's as hard today as it was then. You just have to be slightly different about how you go about putting movies together.

Your first years of producing were with Barry Levinson, one person, one artist. You learned how to protect the vision of one artist.

There was with him supremacy of character in his writings. So I didn't start with somebody who was doing only plot-driven movies. A lot of our movies like *Diner* didn't have, as some said, "anything happening." We had an executive sit down with us and said, "You've got a lot to learn about editing." And Barry said, "Sure it's my first movie, and I'm sure you're right. What do you mean?"

"Well, that scene in the diner with the roast beef, you don't need it." And we were thinking, "But that's the movie." It is two guys sort of bullshitting about who is going to eat a sandwich. If we cut that out, what are we cutting to? We don't have any bank robbery to go to. We don't have any car chases.

I still love that Baltimore Colts test that they gave to their prospective fiancées. The fact that they emphasized knowledge of pro football as essential in a wife was hilarious.

Yes, that was Barry's writing, his knowledge and understanding of these characters, and how they really didn't know anything about women. There were some great things that I learned from Barry, and I will forever be beholden. The important thing is that he was such a good writer and became such an extraordinary director.

There's always been the theory about the auteur, the writer-director. What about a producer as an auteur? You are really putting the elements together. It's your vision of the movie.

I would like to believe that's true, but I don't think so. I'm just in awe of good directors like Barry Levinson. A good director is an extraordinary artist, and I've worked with some really great ones, from Levinson to Clint Eastwood to Alfonso Cuaron. I consider John Lee Hancock a really good filmmaker. I take pride in a lot of what I do, but ultimately the film belongs to the director. I think that a great film has to be made by a great director. There may be one or two exceptions.

I really have always subscribed to the *auteur* theory, and that's why I was affected by the death of Andrew Sarris. When I was a kid, I would read about the *auteur* theory.

There are probably one or two producers you could say that about. There are great producers. I am always in awe of what Jerry Bruckheimer does. You know what you're getting when you go to one of Jerry's movies. I would like to think my name is synonymous with a certain kind of quality, but I don't think it's synonymous with a kind of film. A so-called Mark Johnson production, I don't know if that means anything. Hopefully, it means there is a certain qualitative thing to it.

I read Andrew Sarris' book in which he ranks the directors. He has the pantheon, and you work your way down. He made me realize that there are people like Nicholas Roeg, a whole host of American directors who at first glance you might not value so much. Then you realize what he or she was doing. They have a singular vision, and there's so much to be said about that.

There are directors whose films, no matter what their topics are, whatever world they put you in, you can tell it's their work. With some directors, you can say 30 seconds into the film: "This is a Pedro Almodovar film," "This is a Wes Anderson film."

***You began on a very high note. Your first movie was* A Little Princess.**

A Little Princess is, perhaps, the movie I'm most proud of. But we did not have a lot of money. At one point, we all got vaccinations to go to India and then we realized we didn't have the money to go to India. So we did the whole thing on the Warners lot, which actually turned out to be a blessing. It enabled us to create this entirely not naturalistic rendition of India. It was the idealized world that this little girl thinks about, or can connect to.

It was a movie that I started developing when we adopted my daughter. It was sort of my gift to her. There are so many things wrapped up in it. It's as close to a perfect movie as I'll ever come. It's not perfect by any means, but it's pretty extraordinary. It was great, because Barry and I had just broken up.

It was Alfonso Cuaron whose direction was brilliant. Also, it was shot by Emmanuel Lubezki, one of the best cameramen. We had a wonderful production design and artistic look, which was done by Bo Welch and Cheryl Carasik. It was just a great confluence of wonderful filmmakers. We got a New Generation Award for Alfonso from the Los Angeles Critics Association.

Our reviews were extraordinary from just about everybody. The critics loved it. The first taste I got with that was the Todd McCarthy review in *Variety* that was extraordinary. So many of you critics embraced the movie that when it didn't do business when it first opened, Warner Bros. did the extraordinary thing of opening it again. They opened it twice. Still, it didn't do the business we thought it would do. I spent about six months trying to figure it out. How do I actually fit in here? I can't make a movie better than this, but if it doesn't work for an audience, where have I gone wrong? We then went on to do *Donnie Brasco* and *Galaxy Quest.*

You don't stick to just one genre or type of movie. You are so versatile, and even surprised me when you did a horror movie.
Thank you. And that includes the movies I did with Barry Levinson. They're just different. I think we all try to connect things. If there is a theme in common, it has to do with family, and I think that is important. The family is not necessarily the family that you are born into, but the family you make—the family we surround ourselves with. With people who complete us, who we can rely on. Who will help, who will be there when we stumble.

At that point in my career I was trying to see about going after some private money to finance my company. I went to a trusted agent and he said, "You know what your problem is? You're too varied in your work. You don't just stand for one thing. With some producers you can say, 'He does action really well.'" And I thought, "I think that's a talent." So, I think if you could do big-budget studio films and smaller personal visions, that would be a plus. Anyway, that's what I'm proud of.

I'm like a moviegoer. I like to go see everything. I'm happy with a $200 million franchise movie done well, or I couldn't be happier in a movie theater watching *Beasts of the Southern Wild.* It all depends on how you feel when you wake up that day. Do I want to read Dostoevsky or do I want to pick up something on the Marx Brothers?

How about the finance side? Are you good at it?
Actually, I'm not. I wish I had a business partner to help me with that. I don't think I make particularly good deals. I'm a sucker in that if there's a movie that I want to get made and somebody will make it, I will pretty much give him or her whatever they want.

The beauty of it now is that movies are made in many different ways. In the world I started in and the one that some of my contemporaries mourn for, it was the studio movie. There were so many studios, and that's how you got your movie made. You'd read a script, and say, "This is perfect for Warners," and that's where you'd take it. Now movies are being made in any number of ways. I did a couple of years ago a $900,000 movie called *Ballast*. It won at Sundance as Best Director. Then there are the *Narnia* movies, financed by Walden Media. The first two were distributed by Disney, and the third one was at Fox.

We have a movie called *Bless Me, Alta* based on a book that you and I have never heard of but which is a hugely important book in the Southwest. It's considered the first piece of literary art. It's set in New Mexico in the 1940s. It's about an eight-year-old Hispanic boy, questioning the world in which he lives and the spiritual nature of that world. And, also the rather unique relationship he has with his grandmother. That was completely financed by one person who believed in the book.

The beauty of it is, I don't think I'm a good dealmaker. I'm good at finding a way to get a movie made. If it's through private funding, great. If it's through cobbling together foreign and domestic money, great. I have a very good friend right now who builds Walgreens, among other things, throughout the Southwest. He's a big fan of movies, and he's financed a lot of the development of our films.

You've made some movies from bestsellers, and I've heard you've been trying to get John Grisham's The Testament made. Can you talk about your relationship with the publishing industry?

I have been doing this for a while. I have a pretty good track record with the movies we've made. With one or two exceptions, they've all been successful. A lot of them artistically and almost all of them financially. Also, I have a reputation of being a fair, even-headed person. If I read something that I like, I know how to put it together, secure the rights.

The Testament is a John Grisham book that I've been interested in for over ten years. I have been talking to John Grisham's editor, manager and best friend for some time. It was clear for a while that John Grisham did not want to let it go. It was very personal to him. I think just over the years he was beginning to trust me. He was a big fan of our movie *My Dog Skip*, based on the Southern writer William Morris' novel. He ultimately said, "Okay, let's go do this."

This is a movie that we have financed the development from an independent source. We're actually at a point now where we've got a script, and we're ready to move forward. The narrative is a great blend. That's both a blessing and a curse. Is it a romance set in Brazil, or is it a courtroom drama set in the United States? We can go back and forth.

When you develop someone else's work, particularly, a novel, talk about your input.

I think it happens sometime in the development. There are certain films that I take a great pride in the development of. I think *The Notebook* was one that we had a couple of false starts in terms of writing. I think that I was very helpful in terms of the final editing of the movie, and a little bit in the selling. In terms of key decisions and changes to make, in terms of *The Notebook* we made some big changes from the novel. Nicolas Sparks says that he agrees with the changes we made.

You have a strong story sense. You've adapted a lot of novels into movies.

That's interesting. I used to think that I didn't develop books, that Scott Rudin did the books. But when I think about it, I realize I've done several: *The Natural, Quiz Show, Donnie Brasco*, obviously the *Narnia* movies, *My Dog Skip, The Notebook, My Sister's Keepers*—more than I thought.

I'm always asked: What does a producer do? I can give a sort of set answer: He or she acquires the material, and does this and does that. I think that's all very well and good. What I love about the job is that each film is completely different. The big secret is, experience doesn't count for much. Whatever you learned on the last movie has no application to the next one. So, if you're bright and you're responsive and somewhat inventive, I think that you can produce a movie. There's no big trick to it. Our just going around trying to convince people that we're the only ones who know how to do this is not true.

You must have a strong persistence gene in you.

There's a woman who worked with me years ago. She's very successful now at one of the studios. I read an interview with her recently in which she said one of the things she learned from me was, don't take no for an answer. I hear no all the time. Obviously, I'm disappointed, but it hardly undoes me. If it's something that I believe in, I'm eventually going to find someone who believes in it because I don't think my taste is so unique that nobody else is going to get it. You have to be persistent and stand by your own gut. If you truly think that something's good, sooner or later someone else is going to arrive at that same conclusion. When I go back to *Diner*, I didn't know how to produce a movie, or how to sell a movie, but I did know that Pauline Kael was very powerful, and she was very connected. Our movie was in trouble, so why not do a "Hail Mary" and show it to her. Maybe she would like it as much as I do. And, lo and behold, she did.

JOHNSON'S FILMOGRAPHY

Producer
Cry/Fly (2014)
Bless Me, Ultima (2013)
Not Fade Away (2012)
Won't Back Down (2012)
The Chronicles of Narnia: The Voyage of the Dawn Treader (2010)
Don't Be Afraid of the Dark (2010)
My Sister's Keeper (2009)
The Chronicles of Narnia: Prince Caspian (2008)
The Hunting Party (2007)
How to Eat Fried Worms (2006)
The Chronicles of Narnia: The Lion, the Witch and the Wardrobe (2005)
The Wendell Baker Story (2005)
The Notebook (2004)
The Alamo (2004)
Moonlight Mile (2002)
The Banger Sisters (2002)
The Rookie (2002)
Dragonfly (2002)
An Everlasting Piece (2000)
My Dog Skip (2000)
Galaxy Quest (1999)
Home Fries (1998)
Donnie Brasco (1997)
A Little Princess (1995)
Jimmy Hollywood (1994)
A Perfect World (1993)
Toys (1992)
Bugsy (1991)
Avalon (1990)
Rain Man (1988)
Good Morning, Vietnam (1987)
Tin Men (1987)
Young Sherlock Holmes (1985)
The Natural (1984)

Executive Producer
Last Weekend (2014)
Aloft (2014)

Co-producer
The World of Don Camillo (1984)

Arnold Kopelson

Producer of such acclaimed films as Platoon *and* The Fugitive, *Arnold Kopelson combines a legal background with a passion for movies. Ranging from big-budget action movies to smaller, challenging films, Kopelson's movies have received more than a dozen Oscar nominations—*The Fugitive *was nominated for Best Picture and* Platoon *won Best Picture.*

Kopelson has produced or executive produced 29 motion pictures and was honored as Producer of the Year at ShoWest in 1994. His films are an eclectic group, including Triumph of the Spirit, Firebirds, Seven, Falling Down, Outbreak, Eraser, U.S. Marshals, Devil's Advocate, A Perfect Murder *and* Don't Say a Word.

Kopelson moved from a legal and financial career into producing. He pioneered the practice of pre-sales in motion pictures, and he has written several articles on motion picture financing. He began his career in New York as an entertainment and banking attorney. As a lawyer, he represented banks that lent to the entertainment industry. In 1972, Kopelson and Anne Frieberg (his future wife and co-producer) formed Inter-Ocean Film Sales to represent independent film producers in marketing their films internationally.

While working with Chemical Bank, Kopelson noted that foreign distributors needed access to U.S. movies. He acquired a low-budget indie, The Last Rebel, *starring former Jets quarterback Joe Namath, and started selling the film, getting names of indie film companies around the world. The venture was an immediate success. Kopelson started looking for other movies, and quickly hit pay dirt by licensing* The Apprenticeship of Duddy Kravitz, *starring Richard Dreyfuss. Inter-Ocean Film Sales recognized the growing demand for U.S. films abroad and capitalized on that need during the 1970s and '80s.*

For years Kopelson worked the markets of MIFED, Cannes and the AFM. During the period, Inter-Ocean represented producers of more than 100 motion pictures, including Twice in a Lifetime *and* Salvador. *The company thrived in the 1970s but in the '80s, with sales declining, Kopelson ventured into the production arena. He formed Film Packages Inc. to develop and produce motion pictures. He produced his first three movies with the Boston-based General Cinema Corp. Among his early productions, Kopelson executive-produced* Porky's, *which grossed more than $100 million. More auspiciously, he teamed with Oliver Stone to produce the Vietnam War saga* Platoon *in 1986. His follow-up* Triumph of the Spirit, *the story of a Balkan boxing champion sent to Auschwitz, was praised by Holocaust survivors. Among his other ventures, Kopelson acquired the rights to the TV series* The Fugitive, *which he turned into a blockbuster movie with Harrison Ford as Dr. Richard Kimble. The second highest grossing film in the history of Warner Bros., it was nominated for seven Academy Awards (including Best Picture). Kopelson's first look deal with Warner Bros. resulted in his films earning multiple Academy Award nominations, as well as making in excess of three billion dollars.*

Kopelson signed an exclusive production deal with 20th Century Fox in 1995. In 2004, he and his wife Anne formed a joint venture with Star Farm Productions to turn children's properties into films. Their first project was Edgar & Ellen, *a book series from Simon & Schuster.*

Kopelson was born February 14, 1935, in Brooklyn. His father, a musician, taught him classical piano for over ten years. Although Kopelson had impressive technical ability, his friendships with the extraordinary pianists Van Cliburn, Howard Aibel, and Olegna Fuschi of the Juilliard School made him realize that his talent might be in other endeavors. He earned a Management and Marketing degree from New York University and then received a J.D. degree from New York Law School, while working full time at the prestigious law firm Cravath, Swaine & Moore.

After being admitted to the New York Bar, Kopelson joined the New York law firm of Gettinger & Gettinger, and for ten years represented Chemical Bank and other banks and financial institutions, and became an expert in the financing of motion pictures.

In addition to his Best Picture Oscar, Kopelson has received a Golden Globe from the Hollywood Foreign Press, a Lifetime Achievement in Filmmaking award from the Publicists Guild of America, and many other awards relating to his production activities. He also received the

New York Law School Distinguished Alumnus Award for Lifetime Achievement.

Kopelson serves on the executive committee of the Producers Branch of the Academy of Motion Picture Arts and Sciences. He is a member of the Board of Mentors of the Peter Stark Motion Picture program at USC. On March 27, 2007, he became a member of the Board of Directors of CBS Corporation.

Duane Byrge: What are you if you say you are a producer?

Arnold Kopelson: Being a producer is about a few things—it's passion, it's persistence, it's determination and it's a belief in what you are doing. You don't go into any project unless you thoroughly believe in it. It's a different level of involvement when you have the passion, as I did on *The Fugitive*. You just have to stay with it and make it happen.

Anne Kopelson and I are very much a team. She didn't want to receive screen credit on the earlier films I produced but has been with me every step of the way. We produce all films and television together as a team.

Following graduation from law school, I joined the New York Law firm of Gettinger & Gettinger as an associate. The firm represented banks, as did the firm of Cravath, Swaine & Moore, where I previously was employed. There were over 300 applicants for the position, but when they heard that I had been at the Cravath firm for three years, I was given the position. My entering salary was $75 a week and I was happy when I received a raise to $100 a week.

Because I was used to working day and night at Cravath—I used to keep a blanket at the job and work

Arnold Kopelson, 2015. Courtesy Arnold Kopelson.

all night long—that they made me a partner in Gettinger & Gettinger in two years. That started me in the movie area because they really wanted to be the first law firm that created banking for movies. That was unheard of at the time.

I was assigned to represent the Chemical Bank in their motion picture lending division. In a short time, I began representing other banks and financial institutions in movie financing and developed an expertise in this area of law. At the same time, I was taking on additional clients who came to me thinking that because I represented banking institutions I could get them bank loans. The fact is that banks only lend money to those that have good credit. However, I was able to assist borrowers in structuring their requests to make them bankable. Through this experience, I developed as interest in the movie business.

On a trip abroad with a client, I was repeatedly asked by distributors in foreign countries to find them films for distribution. The independent distributors as distinguished from the major studios distribution subsidiaries, owned the theaters and could give the best playtime to films which they acquired. They owned hundreds of theaters and they wanted films from me. So I came back and said to Anne, who was then my legal secretary, "We've got to find a movie, there's definitely a need for movies."

So I got [a copy of *The Last Rebel*]. It was distributed in North America by Columbia. No one wanted it in the foreign market. I did some research with the Merchant Association of America as to what each country would be worth and the overall worth. I came out with the amount of money I would likely get out of this.

We didn't have e-mails then, no faxing either. I sent out a brochure called a pressbook by ordinary mail, with quotes of what I thought each country should pay for the rights. I basically forgot about it. After a while I started to receive checks which totaled more than I had received for any single year practicing law.

I said to Anne, "I think we have a business. [Let's] set up a company and let's acquire more movies for distribution." We called it Inter-Ocean Film Sales, Ltd. I was introduced to the great Italian film director, Sergio Leone. He had created the spaghetti Westerns which had been hugely successful. Leone needed a representative to sell his films and was able to license *My Name Is Nobody*, starring Henry Fonda, to various foreign countries, and in the United States I made a deal with Universal Pictures. My deal with Leone was that I would receive ten percent.

That was a very interesting experience because Leone wanted $3 million for the U.S. rights and a few territories. I called Hy Martin, who was chairman of Universal distribution. He said they were interested. I had a ten percent deal with Leone, and I needed the money. Later I got a call from Martin when I was having lunch with Anne. He said, "Arnold, I am really sorry, we priced that out, and we are going to pass. We can't pay more than $2,750,000." We were very close.

Then, it was like a light went on in my head. I said, "I'm going to call Leone." Sergio spoke no English, so I called his cousin, Fulvio Morsella, who was Sergio's partner and acted as his interpreter. When Fulvio got on the phone I said that Hy Martin, the president of Universal, wants to come to Rome to meet with Sergio. He held the phone while he told Sergio what I said. Sergio said he would be delighted to meet with Mr. Martin. I called back Hy Martin and told him that Sergio would like to meet with him in Rome. Hy said he was going to London and would be happy to meet with Sergio in Rome.

So Sergio Leone thought that the Universal executive had flown to Rome specifically to meet him?

Yes, but I had to figure out how I was going to get there. I had no money. I had to use Anne's credit card. So I flew to Rome on Anne's card. The ego of Sergio was so great that the fact the person at Universal came to see him that he consented to the deal within ten minutes. I made over $200,000 on that.

Getting to be a producer, you not only have to fly by the seat of your pants, but it obviously helps if you can fly on your secretary's credit card.

Well, you have to be creative and think on your feet. You have to be willing to take risks. And have a great partner.

There are general crises with every film, whether in the very beginning or various stages. *The Fugitive* is one great example of that. I was involved in keeping it alive, fighting for it, draft after draft, staying with it and knowing that it was right. It's a long story, as all stories are about how movies eventually get made. It goes way back to when I developed a movie called *Wings of the Apache*, where I had formed a joined venture with Keith Barish. Keith was promoting me because he thought I had money, and I was promoting him because I thought he had money for making movies. It was really funny—we both thought the other guy had money. Keith called me one day and said he was leaving his studio arrangement. He said he had the choice of either taking a script called *The Flintstones* or *The Fugitive*. Which one would you like?

I couldn't believe I was hearing this. It was maybe ten years before that when I was leaving the practice of law that I called Quinn Martin, who was a client of the firm. We were doing his banking, and I had been involved in some of his transactions. I said, "Quinn, I am about to be a movie producer, and I would like to do *The Fugitive*." He told me my instincts were very good, but I was too late. He had made a deal already. So, ten years later, I got the rights back. I couldn't believe it. It was my dream. So I started to develop the project with Keith. He stayed six months and lost interest, but stayed on with the title of executive producer. He was mainly in the real estate business. He had done a couple of movies but really didn't get into it.

I worked on it for five and a half years through 25 different drafts of the screenplay written by nine writers. Finally Warner Bros., which had spent $2 million on writers' fees, had lost confidence in the project and put it in turnaround [dropped the project] for a period of two weeks, giving another person the right to set it up elsewhere if they could give them back the $2 million. They did not succeed and I said to the president of production, "Now let me make my film." He said okay, so I went back to my first writer.

I sent that draft to Pat McQueeney, Harrison Ford's agent, and she got back to me and said that Harrison wanted to do the movie and would like to meet with me. I met with Harrison at the Warner Bros commissary, and we discussed the film for over two hours. Every few minutes I wanted to pinch myself, as I couldn't believe I was meeting with the most successful actor in the movie business, and he wanted my opinion on various parts of the script. Harrison committed to play Dr. Richard Kimble at that meeting.

Harrison wanted to know who would direct. At a Warner Bros. screening of *Under Siege*, directed by Andy Davis, I walked over to Bob Daly and Terry Semel, who had just seen the film, and I said that Andy

Davis should direct *The Fugitive*. They agreed. I then walked over to Bruce Berman, the president of production, and told him that Bob and Terry had approved Andy to direct *The Fugitive*. Bruce said, "Great." I then walked over to Andy and told him that he should be in my office on Monday morning as he had been approved to direct *The Fugitive*. In the interim, I got Harrison to approve Andy. Jeb Stuart became our ninth and final writer.

When we went to make the movie, no one realized that we didn't have a viable third act. The third act that was written had a car going into the subway and chasing the train along the rails. It was not doable as no one gave any thought as to how a car could get past the turnstile of the train. We had to rewrite the entire third act because of this. So we get up to production, and we still didn't have a third act. We started the movie, and the trains are rolling, literally. Every night right after the shooting we would go to our hotel room. Bob Brassel, who was at Warner Bros., Andy, Harrison, Peter Macgregor-Scott, Jeb Stuart and I would attempt to block out the next scene. Harrison would act it out for Andy, and then Jeb would write the scene.

After the movie was finished, Harrison was in total despair. He didn't think it worked. When he saw it for the first time, he cried. He thought it was great.

I remember we were sitting around waiting for the results, and we got the highest preview score Warner Bros. had ever gotten. All that from having been told earlier by them that I was wasting my time and money.

Tell us about Platoon. *That was an extremely difficult project to get made.*

Platoon had been around for ten years. Oliver [Stone] had started filming it before, but he never got anywhere. He wrote it after he had gotten out of Vietnam. He had been wounded twice and started to peddle it. He took it everywhere.

Gerald Green called me one day and asked me if I knew who Oliver Stone was. Of course I did. Oliver had just won an Academy Award for his screenplay of *Midnight Express*. He told me that he had Stone's script on the Vietnam War. I said I wanted to see it immediately. [Prior to that] I had been rejecting anything on Vietnam—I didn't want to get involved in it. But this was the tenth anniversary of the ending of the war. They were building the Vietnam Memorial. My independent distributors abroad were looking for an action movie, a war movie.

I gave the script to each of my kids. One was in college, one was in high school, and one was in grade school. My college son said his history class on Vietnam was his best elective in college. My son in high school said, "We know nothing about Vietnam. It's not even in our history book." He encouraged me to make it. And my young daughter came back and said her friends would want to watch this movie.

So I started reading the script. I read about 50 pages and I called Oliver. I said, "I've got to produce this." He said, "Not so fast. Go home and finish the script." So I went home that night and while I was in bed, I was reading and reading. I was perspiring. At the end of the script, I was sobbing. Anne asked me what was wrong. I told her that I had just read the finest screenplay I had ever read, and that while I was reading it I had a full fantasy of winning an Academy Award. I told her, "We'll never get closer." Anne asked if it would make money. Anne handles the business affairs of our company. I said that I wasn't sure, but I had to produce this movie. I will have to go to somewhere in the Far East for about three months. Anne said I should follow my instincts.

So I called Oliver and I said, "I really want to do this film." We ended up forming a film venture between us, it was 50–50. I then started to place the movie. There was a general concern: was it going to make money? I had no idea. But I saw greatness in the script. Before this happened, [Orion] didn't want to make *Platoon*. At the time, we were involved in raising money for *Salvador*, which Oliver was filming, and Orion was set to distribute. There was a lot of concern from investors because people weren't sure if he could direct. Anne and I went down to Cuernavaca and Acapulco, Mexico, where *Salvador* was being filmed. We watched Oliver directing for two weeks and saw the dailies and went back to Los Angeles, and we told them that not only can he direct, he is a great director.

Then Orion said they weren't going to get involved in *Platoon* unless Oliver agreed to make eight cuts in *Salvador*. Oliver didn't understand how violent the movie was. There was a scene depicting a female officer making six prisoners get down on their knees in an execution position. She then blew their heads off. Oliver had one take where you actually see the man's face blown off his head.

We screened the footage in Milan, and we did not know what we would see. There were 200 people in the screening room. There were screams when that shot came on screen and two women passed out. I called Oliver back in America and told him that it was too violent. He said, "That's not violent. I was shot twice in Vietnam, and that was violent." Oliver was resisting making cuts in the film, and Orion wouldn't put up the money for *Platoon* unless he made the cuts. Putting on my legal hat, I prepared a document specifying the cuts that he had to make, and Oliver signed off, and we had the money for *Platoon*.

My legal background was a very big help with some productions. When I first started out, I segued from law to moviemaking. In my early days, I found out that General Cinema Corporation had been producing Lew Grade movies, and they were not happy with the result. So I decided to take a shot at it. I called the chairman of the General Cinemas Corporation, which was a big public company at the time, and I went to see him. I told him I was in banking and wanted to produce films with them. He said my time couldn't have been better. Being a big company, they thoroughly researched my background. They did something like an FBI search on my background, and they ended up giving me $31 million to make three movies with them, which I did.

Outbreak is another story of how I utilized my strategy skills. I was developing a project based on the book *Crisis in the Hot Zone*. It was a tremendous, exciting book about a virus that was spreading. We had Dustin Hoffman, Morgan Freeman and Renee Russo. Plus, I had signed a very talented director, Wolfgang Petersen, who had made *Das Boot*. I was trying to get a script and a writer. We went to many studios.

You were putting it all together without a completed script?

I knew that Fox was making *Crisis in the Hot Zone* with Robert Redford and Jodie Foster. So there were going to be two movies developed with very similar themes. They were ready to start shooting their movie, but we weren't ready to start. It was weeks away from starting, but I knew that I had to catch the position on this movie. So I developed a strategy that was based on my years of legal strategy and litigation.

I announced we were going to move the company up to Northern California, and that production had begun. I wanted it to be on the front page of *The Hollywood Reporter*'s International Edition on Tuesday.

Was that true?

Yes, it was true. We shot second unit material, but it went all out all over the world that we had begun.

You first established your name with Porky's, which was passed over by the studios at the time but became a forerunner of today's raunchy teen comedies. It's quite a stretch from Porky's to Platoon.

It was a very funny script, and I was doing low-budget movies at the time. Bob Clark came to me after I had done those movies, because Bob had apparently heard I had been successful in working with low-budget productions. He came to me with about five or six properties. One of them was *Porky's*, which sounded absolutely hysterical. The script was very funny. I asked, "How much money do you need to get this done?" He said about $10,000. I gave him my own money, which is something I had never done before. I would produce the movie, and he would direct it. On that investment, I eventually made $2 million.

When I was embarking on it, trying to raise more money for the production, I called a friend of mine, Jeff [Katzenberg], at Paramount. I said, "Listen, I have a script called *Porky's*. It's a coming-of-age comedy, very sexy." He said, "Send it over." I told him I wasn't going to have him give it to one of his assistants to read. If he wanted it, he would have to come to my place and read it himself. He came up to the house one afternoon, and he read the script. He said it was the funniest script he had ever read, but said, "You expect Paramount to distribute this film when a guy is sticking his dick through a wall?" While still laughing, he passed. Later, when it opened, Jeffrey called me and said, "I am taking you guys to dinner. Saying no to *Porky's* was the greatest mistake I've made here."

You definitely take creative risks, not only in launching a production before you had a completed script, but you've taken projects that have been considered very risky material.

120

Again, it's related to being passionate about something. *Seven* was another script that I had read, and I was overwhelmed by it. It was so powerful. I found out that the rights had been all screwed up. There was a producer who had been on it for three years and had done nothing. There were others in the mix.

My legal training gave me the ability to pull together all of the pieces. The person who had the project for three years was given a producer credit, and I was able to give the Italian company the distribution rights for Italy, and I gave an executive producer credit to one of its employees. I brought the cleaned-up project to New Line. I then brought in David Fincher, who was virtually unemployable at the time, but I believed in him and his ability. I then brought Brad Pitt, Morgan Freeman and Kevin Spacey to the project, and we made our movie for approximately $30 million. It became a major success and still remains in distribution in various parts of the world and on television and other platforms, approximately 20 years after its first release.

It is remarkable how you revive projects and keep them going.
That's the main part of producing, starting out with something that no one necessarily wants to do and then bringing it to the screen. You have to overcome all the problems that invariably come up. As I've said, it's passion and it's persistence.

One of my favorite films of yours was* Falling Down, *which I have to believe must have been very difficult to get made.
That's true but it came together following my bringing Joel Schumacher into the project. At Warner Bros., Bruce Berman thought Joel was a good choice, but Bob Daly and Terry Semel were not very keen on his directing it. I got behind him and convinced them that he was the right person for the project. I liked Joel because he has a great eye. He came with a background in design. He used to create department stores windows in the big stores in New York. He did wonderful set designs.

Joel and I hit it off. He said he was going to Santa Barbara for the weekend. When he was there, he gave Michael Douglas the script at his home. He came back Monday morning and said that Michael was willing to do the movie. That was absolutely amazing. So it came together. It was amazing that it could be made because it was really a downer story. It was a hard film that way.

When we were on the set the first day at Santa Monica, we were actually beginning to film the last scene of the picture, where Michael gets shot. We were just about ready to shoot the scene when the phone rang for Joel. It was Terry Semel. When Joel got off the phone he said, "You are not going to believe this, but Terry just said, 'I am just looking on what you guys are about to make, and I wish you could come up with a more consumer-friendly ending.'" We were going to shoot that scene in less than three minutes. Joel had said to Terry, "We will try to come up with something, but if you can come up with something better, we will shoot it." We shot it the way it was written, and I think it's Michael's best film to date.

As I've said, it takes passion and determination, but it's always been worth it. I love the business, and it's hard to believe that I am doing this. It's tough to make movies, but I am so thrilled to be able to do it. I get up every morning, and I love what I do. I can't wait to get started.

KOPELSON'S FILMOGRAPHY

Producer
Twisted (2004)
Joe Somebody (2001)
Don't Say a Word (2001)
A Perfect Murder (1998)
U.S. Marshals (1998)
The Devil's Advocate (1997)
Mad City (1997)
Eraser (1996)
Seven (1995)
Outbreak (1995)
The Fugitive (1993)
Falling Down (1993)
Out for Justice (1997)

Murder at 1600 (1997)
Triumph of the Spirit (1989)
Platoon (1986)

Executive Producer
Firebirds (1990)
Warlock (1989)
Gimme an "F" (1984)
Porky's (1982)
Dirty Tricks (1981)
Final Assignment (1980)
Night of the Juggler (1980)
Lost and Found (1979)
The Legacy (1978)

Alan Ladd Jr.

Completely unlike the stereotypical studio chief or producer, Alan Ladd Jr. is widely respected in the entertainment industry for his movie savvy and quiet decency. Affectionately called "Laddie" by peers and friends, he is genial and soft-spoken. During the course of his multi-faceted career, he served as president of Twentieth Century Fox, as well as chairman and CEO of MGM/UA.

The son of legendary actor Alan Ladd, he is known for making tasteful, commercial pictures. The Ladd Company produced Braveheart *and* Chariots of Fire, *both Best Picture Oscar winners. In all, Ladd's films have won more than 150 Oscars.*

Formed in 1979 with his former Fox associates Jay Kanter and Gareth Wigan, the Ladd Company also produced Night Shift, Police Academy, The Right Stuff, The Phantom, The Brady Bunch Movie, A Very Brady Sequel *and the noir thriller* Body Heat, *winner of the Los Angeles Film Critics Association Best Film honor in 1983.*

In high school, Ladd worked part-time as a movie usher so he could watch Errol Flynn pictures five or six times each. He developed his "Saturday Matinee Rule of Thumb" for a movie: the audience must root for the hero and boo the bad guy, and the story must move quickly.

After high school graduation, he studied abroad for a year and a half while his father was making movies in Europe. He returned to Los Angeles and enrolled at the University of Southern California. Ladd began his movie career as a stunt man during a summer vacation from USC. He landed his first full-time job in the movie industry in 1963 as a motion picture talent agent with Creative Management Associates, where he represented Judy Garland, among others.

Six years later, he turned to independent production and moved to London, where he produced nine films over a four-year period. He returned to Los Angeles in 1973 to become head of creative affairs for 20th Century Fox. After advancing to vice-president of production in

1974, and senior vice-president of worldwide production in 1975, Ladd became president of Twentieth Century Fox in 1976.

During his tenure, the studio produced some of the most successful films in its history, including Star Wars, *which he optioned after Universal rejected it. He championed* Star Wars *against the wishes of his board, and the film became the most profitable in Fox history at the time.*

Due to his low-key guidance and passion for movies, Fox became known as the "filmmaker's studio." Ladd championed lower-budget projects that made Fox the most adventurous studio of the decade. He had the insight and confidence to give boosts to such maverick filmmakers as Robert Altman and Paul Mazursky.

Before it was fashionable, Ladd supported films about women: Three Women, Julia, The Turning Point, An Unmarried Woman *and* Norma Rae. *Having shown that the general public would be receptive to female protagonists, he upped the ante by making a woman the main protagonist in the big-budget action film* Alien, *starring Sigourney Weaver.*

Under his tenure, Hollywood had its first female vice-president, Paula Weinstein, and its first black marketing chief, Ashley Boone. He was also innovative in terms of distribution, pioneering the select-site release pattern.

Ladd resigned from Fox in 1979, out of frustration with the stifling corporate strictures of chairman Dennis Stanfill, a former investment banker with Lehman Bros. They clashed, among other things, over Ladd's wish to include lower-level executives in bonus positions.

In 1985 Ladd joined MGM/UA, where he served as chairman and chief executive until 1988. While there, he was responsible for Spaceballs, Willow, Moonstruck, *and* A Fish Called Wanda. *Under Ladd, the once-sickly lion roared again.*

He next moved to Pathé Entertainment, where he served as chairman and chief executive officer. In 1991, Ladd was hired by Italian financier Giancarlo Parretti to head MGM/UA. He developed risky films such as Thelma & Louise. *When Parretti was ousted in May 1992, Ladd took the reins. But he was shackled by the shabby ministrations of Credit Lyonais. The French bankers ousted Ladd in 1993. When Ladd served notice he would file a breach-of-contract lawsuit, he was reportedly* *given $10 million to walk away. Additionally, he was allowed to take with him certain projects, which included* Braveheart. *Ladd then re-established the Ladd Company through a production deal with Paramount Pictures.*

Braveheart'*s Best Picture Oscar was in a sense a payback for Ladd. His acceptance of the Academy Award generated a heartfelt standing ovation from fellow Academy members: For them, Alan Ladd Jr. was someone to root for.*

Duane Byrge: What is the first thing a producer does?

Alan Ladd Jr.: First you have to start with a script. Finding the script is the most important thing. Then you have to get the right director. Next, you do the casting. Everything starts from a script. It goes from there. You get a story and assemble a team.

The best producers love movies. That's all I did, see movie after movie as a kid. Of course, they had double features in those days. You get so you can identify who shot it, or directed. You got to know who were the top directors—that kind of thing.

I still like those kinds of Saturday matinee movies. They were great. I went through a period of going to the movies on Saturdays. It was fun. As a kid, I didn't like Joan Crawford or Bette Davis, but I still went. I saw the movies, and I saw that they were popular. I realized there was a big audience of women out there.

Today, it seems there's not as much respect for story or narrative. It's often just special effects driving the story.

Exactly. You walk out of the theater and say, "What was that movie all about?" Or today an *Indi-*

Alan Ladd Jr., 2014. Courtesy Alan Ladd Jr.

ana Jones sequel gets reviewed badly and you say, "Wait a minute, they are just making entertainment. They are not trying to show us Shakespeare." That's what George [Lucas] had in mind when he set out to make *Star Wars*. He was not intending to win Academy Awards. He just wanted to make a great entertainment.

At USC you majored in business administration, not cinema.

Yes, I did. People said, "You should go to cinema school," but the cinema school was in a tiny little shack. In business administration, they had nice classrooms, so that's what I studied. All through college I continued to see movies every day. I didn't study hard. I spent all my time at the movies. There used to be all these pictures at the Nuart Theatre or at the museums. That was before the cable channels and Turner Classic Movies.

You rescued Mel Brooks' movie Young Frankenstein.

Mel had done *The Producers*, which was a very successful movie. He was developing *Young Frankenstein* at Columbia. The producer was a close friend of mine, Frank Price. I read the script. It was hysterical. So I went over to the studio. That's when Columbia and Warner Bros. were both at the Burbank lot. I met Mel at the cutting room. He had just shown it to Warner Bros. They weren't going to release the movie. Except for one executive, they all hated it. They thought it was disgusting and horrible.

I saw it with a preview audience, and the crowd went nuts. I didn't agree with the studio that it was disgusting. I took it to the head of distribution at Fox at that time, Bobby Littman. He said that Warner Bros had just put it in turnaround. They wanted to make it for $1.8 million, and they said it was going to cost $1.9 million, so they didn't want to make it. I said, "If they're not doing it, let's jump on it right away." So he did, and we made the deal that day. We paid Mel at the time. It wasn't too much. It came out, and it did very well.

You've got to like all kinds of movies, or appreciate the different types of audiences. A good example is the *Police Academy* movies. We didn't make them to win awards but because we thought they were funny. A lot of people like that kind of comedy.

When did you first think you wanted to be a producer?
It never entered my mind. I never had a goal to be a producer.
I got out of the service, and I was looking for a job, but there were
no jobs. I was a stunt man for a while, but I was just a college kid when
I did it. I worked for the Coast Guard and at gas stations. I never
thought about producing, not for a minute, or being involved as an
executive.

I didn't know what to do. I asked Mattie Racht, who used to be
head of Paramount Studios, for advice. I knew that he was a very sincere
and responsible guy. He said that I should become an agent. I took his
advice. I interviewed at a couple of agencies. I interviewed at MCA,
which had just started up. They said, "Well, we don't really have anything," but they called me a little later and they said they needed a secretary. So I worked there as a secretary.

Then Freddie Fields' secretary called me and said, "Mr. Fields has
a job for you, but it only pays $35 a week, and we know you have a
child." I said, "I'm very fortunate that I have a working wife who is a
dental hygienist." I took the job. During the time I was doing my job
there at the agency, they said none of their agents would do television. I said, "Look, why don't I cover television? We have all these
comics and they all want to be actors. So why not try?" They said to
go ahead.

As luck would have it, they were just starting the *Chrysler Theatre.*
They started paying more for top spots, and they paid more for the
top-of-the-show. They paid $25,000—that was years ago. That was a
lot of money. You work for a week, it's $400,000. Not surprisingly,
people started saying, "Yeah, I will do it." As time went on, people like
Steve McQueen were breaking out of TV. Through that, I became a
movie agent.

***Working with the shows' producers must have given you an
insight into the way they thought.***
Exactly. You do this, and do that. You go to the directors and producers of the show and tell them why you think that your particular
client could do the show. Or how could they just change it, fit the role
a little bit. It was a real education. So you thought like they would: How
do I slide my client in? Try to get the right person for the job. Then I

moved from television to features. It was the same thing with feature scripts. You would tell them why you thought your client would be good for the feature.

It was a wonderful education because in those days agents didn't sit in their offices all day. They went to the studios every day. You would meet all the various producers, directors, writers along the particular line you were covering. Now agents just sit down in their office and make phone calls. I got a full movie business education getting to know all these people. After a while you know everybody in town.

You begin thinking you can put a team together. Then you try to put a package together. Packaging is the same as producing or being a studio head. It's all the same. When you are a studio head, you are like a producer's producer.

When you were a studio head, what would you say were the best qualities in the producers that you admired?

The producers I admired the most were people who stuck with the project as opposed to producers who set it up and then you don't see them again till the premiere or something. I never admired those kinds of producers—there are an awful lot of them around town. They make the deal, and then they are gone. I believe a producer should stay with the project, stay on top of it, watch the budget, make suggestions, and do all of that. A producer should do a lot more than just make the deal safe, and don't say, "Oh, I have my money, now I'm done."

Tell us about Braveheart. _That faced a lot of obstacles: period piece, big budget._

I had read a script when I was at MGM on the Scottish hero William Wallace, which I was very impressed with. So I met with Randy [Wallace]. It was called _Braveheart_. I thought his script was terrific. So, I sent it to Mel Gibson, who passed because he was about to do another movie. When I left MGM, as part of my settlement I got to take two projects with me, and _Braveheart_ was one of them. I took it with me to Paramount because I liked the writing.

I was sitting in my office at Paramount one day, and I got a call from Mel. He said, "That script I read a year or so ago, I can't get it out of my head. What are you doing with it?" I told him I had done nothing

128

with it. It was just sitting there. So we met, and he said, "I want to direct it. I don't want to act in it. I just want to direct it."

I didn't want him as a director. I wanted him as an actor. However, if he wanted to direct, that was fine with me. I have worked with a lot of [first-time and] second-time directors. I have always thought that a smart actor can make a good director. I finally agreed, but I said, "You've got to get the actor." He came up with a couple of names. I said, "Well, if you get so-and-so, you're not going to have a battle scene with this person playing it." Finally he said, "I'd like to play it." So that's how the picture got made, and I would give him all the credit.

Before we shot it, Mel and I just talked about it. I was not the director so it was not my part to tell him how to shoot it. Some producers come on the set, and they want to show that power. You have to let the directors have their head up. I trusted him, but I also thought, "I hope to God he knows what he's doing." I later went to him and I said, "Mel, you should take a producer credit." He asked why, and I said, "Because you devoted yourself to this project: You did all the work. You didn't take any calls from the agents. I didn't see you read any other scripts. You were totally immersed in this project, and you were not up for anything else. So, it's something you deserve." He said, "Well, thank you."

How difficult is it dealing with the studios during shooting?

There were problems with *The Right Stuff*. The director [Philip Kaufman] was making a "masterpiece." We kept shooting and shooting. I have never seen the finished product. Warner Bros. never asked a question during the shooting, which went on and on. Yet, Bob [Daly] and Terry [Semel] surely had to wonder, but they didn't say anything. They were pretty tolerant.

Have you experienced other situations where you thought the project was getting out of control?

I had a situation with a picture called *Brubaker*. Bob Rafelson was the director, and he didn't want a movie star. We had Robert Redford playing the lead role of the warden. After the first week of shooting, everything we got back was so dark. You could hardly see Redford. Then I got a call that Rafelson had hit someone on the set. I was going to Indiana to check on *Breaking Away*, so I stopped off in Ohio where we were shooting the picture at an old prison. I found out it was true about the incident. I got angry and fired him, just like that. You can't let anybody get away with that kind of behavior. I had to talk with Robert Redford.

I stayed at his house on location, and I tried to convince him to stay in the picture. It took a lot of convincing. He was getting a lot of pressure from others not to stay. So I said, "We have to get out of town." We went home to Los Angeles and talked about directors.

I wanted to know what he thought about Stuart Rosenberg. He said early in his career he worked on a *Defenders*, and he had a lot of respect for Rosenberg. So he agreed to stay on. It took about a week, I guess. We shut production down for about a week, and then Rosenberg re-shot what had been done up till then. We hung in there and finished the movie successfully.

You did something very unusual: You left as president of 20th Century Fox when you were on top. I don't think anyone has ever done that.

It had become too corporate. I was dealing with people who didn't understand the movie business at all. They had a certain mentality: They wanted profits. They wanted more blockbusters. [Chairman Dennis Stanfill] and I didn't get along well. He was extremely corporate, and I wasn't corporate.

I just didn't see eye to eye with these corporate, studio executives. All directors were supposed to wear a tie. Everybody wore a tie. I dressed a little bit less than I was supposed to. I wore shirts and slacks. We were always filling out reports. And on these reports, they would ask things like, "What did you do to further the profits of this company?"

I'd say I canceled a movie in the middle of production. We would spend one million dollars on it, and by the time we finished we would have spent three million. Then we could have spent two million to market it. So I canceled it and saved the company a lot of money.

That must have confounded the corporate guys.

It did. I was tired of it. I said to myself, "Let me get out of this *Star Wars* business."

You have green-lit or produced a wide array of movies. Any that you don't do?

I love movies, but I won't do horror films. I don't know how to do that kind of movie. I do things that I like, which begins with a good script, obviously. From there, hopefully, you can put it together to get it made. If I don't get who I want, I say to myself, "Don't beat your head against the wall any more."

Your last movie **Gone Baby Gone** *was from a Dennis Lehane novel.*

We had bought the book from a development fund I had at Paramount. Ben Affleck found out about it and asked if he could write the screenplay adaptation. He was writing the script and writing it and writing it. It went on forever. I started a movie with Jennifer Lopez, *Unfinished Life*, which was shooting in Vancouver, and he would come up there. I saw him in Vancouver and I said, "Ben, where is the script?" He didn't have it. Finally I wrote him a letter and said, "If you don't turn the thing in by a certain day, we are going to end it." He came up with a script, and I liked it.

But then Paramount put it in turnaround, so Ben called me and said, "If I can set it up in 24 hours, can I direct it?" I said, "Sure, if you can get it set up, you can direct." He called me a couple hours later and said, "I made a deal with Disney for Miramax." We were off to the races. He directed it, and it was good. Ben has talent, and he's smart too.

You started in 1963 at a talent agency, and now it's 2013. This is your 50th year in the business. Do you realize you have hit a milestone?

No, I didn't realize that. I never even thought about it. Now that you mention it, there's a certain symmetry. The agency where I started was located in this very building where I now have my office, 9255 Sunset. We were originally on the sixth floor when I started.

And now you're on the same floor. You're back where you started.

[*Laughs*] Yes, like at MGM. When I came back there, I discovered I came back to the same office that I had left. I've been lucky and had my shares of success.

Would you go into this business now?

No. When I went into the agency business, it was very different from now. You were friends with the guys at William Morris, friends with people at other agencies. We worked very closely with one another. There wasn't the games-playing. We were honest with one another. When I was a producer, it was the same thing. People would help you, and not sabotage what you were doing. You could work with the studio people also. You could call, say, John Calley and ask, "Is it true you're trying to buy this project for $300,000?" And he'd say, "Yes, it's true." Now people lie to each other. So it doesn't have that kind of familiarity you used to have. The movie world was very close-knit at that time, not any more. Now if you call about something, there are about 20 people you have to go through. So if I was starting all over again. I would not want to be in this business the way it is now. It's become more of a dog-eat-dog business.

Today, decisions are made by lawyers and marketers. They don't know anything about making movies. They don't care really about movies. They are just numbers people. Their idea of input is to say, "Well, you should get Tom Cruise and Brad Pitt." People just make uninformed decisions. They could not care less about the movie. It's just a product to them. Now they get a rise out of cheating someone out of something. It's very different. That was one of the things that I was always pretty good about, I wanted everybody to get their share. I never got sued once.

It's very different today. I was very lucky to have the freedom to pick and choose what I wanted to do and what decisions I would make. I had total freedom on that.

What do you see as a positive in today's production world?

One thing I do know is that there will be new and different venues. New technologies, like Blu-ray. All the libraries are recycling. It's a big world out there. Things get recycled over and over, and there will be new deliveries, like sky television. There will be something else, there's always something else, and there's always room for good stories.

LADD'S FILMOGRAPHY

Producer
Gone Baby Gone (2007)
An Unfinished Life (2005)
A Very Brady Sequel (1996)
The Phantom (1996)
Braveheart (1995)
Zee and Co. (1972)
Fear Is the Key (1972)
Villain (1971)

A Severed Head (1970)
Tam Lin (1970)
The Walking Stick (1970)

Executive Producer
The Man in the Iron Mask (1998)
The Brady Bunch Movie (1995)
Vice Versa (1998)

Michael London

After ten years as a senior production executive and studio producer, Michael London decided to cut his studio ties and set up shop as an independent producer. So, in 1998 he left as executive vice-president of production at 20th Century Fox, where he had supervised the production of Alien 3, Die Hard 2, Sleeping with the Enemy, Hoffa, The Sandlot *and more.*

As an independent producer, his first inclination was to look for books to be adapted into movies. He began by optioning Sideways, *an unpublished novel by a personal friend, Rex Pickett. London produced the Alexander Payne film* Sideways, *which won a Golden Globe for Best Picture (comedy or musical) and an Independent Spirit Award. Oscar-wise it earned a Best Picture nomination, and won for Best Adapted Screenplay.*

While attempting to get Sideways *off the ground, London produced his first two films for Working Title,* The Guru *and* 40 Days and 40 Nights. *He followed up with two noteworthy films in 2003,* Thirteen *and* House of Sand and Fog.

Thirteen *starred Holly Hunter and Evan Rachel Wood and got an enthusiastic reaction at Sundance. London sold the worldwide distribution rights to Fox Searchlight.*

In 2004 London signed a three-year, first-look feature production deal with Paramount with an aim to bridging the gap between major studio projects and specialty indie fare. His first Paramount film The Family Stone *was written and directed by Thomas Bezucha and starred Diane Keaton, Dermot Mulroney and Sarah Jessica Parker.*

London also produced The Illusionist, *a period romantic thriller set in Vienna, starring Edward Norton, Paul Giamatti and Jessica Biel. London teamed up with Alexander Payne to produce* King of California *with Michael Douglas and Evan Rachel Wood.*

In 2006 London formed Groundswell Productions, an independent production and financing company. Its mission was to establish itself *as a creative and stimulating home for filmmakers. Groundswell was backed by two equity-based film funds and was positioned to make five films a year with budgets under $20 million.*

The company's slate mixed established directors and emerging talents, alongside genre films with an original sensibility. The difference between Groundswell and most other equity-based companies was that the films were green-lit by London and not the businessmen. The plan was to cover three-quarters of the budget with a studio advance and a foreign sales agreement.

In 2007, Groundswell premiered Tom McCarthy's The Visitor *at the Toronto Film Festival. Groundswell's films also include* Milk, *directed by Gus Van Sant and starring Sean Penn;* Appaloosa, *directed by Ed Harris, who starred opposite Renee Zellweger; and* The Marc Pease Experience, *which starred Ben Stiller and Jason Schwartzman. Other Groundswell films include* Smart People *and* The Mysteries of Pitts-

From left to right: Producer Michael London on the set of *Trumbo* (2015) with actors Louis C.K. and Bryan Cranston.

burgh, *both of which played at Sundance. London also produced Tom McCarthy's* Win Win *starring Paul Giamatti.*

London was honored as Producer of the Year at the 2006 Palm Springs International Film Festival.

London began his career as a reader at ICM and then segued to journalism as a staff writer for the Los Angeles Times' *Calendar section. His writing attracted the attention of producer Don Simpson, who got London to sign on as a development executive for Simpson-Bruckheimer. While there he worked on* Top Gun *and* Beverly Hills Cop II.

Duane Byrge: You never set out to be a producer.

Michael London: After college, I came to Los Angeles with the vague idea of becoming a serious writer. I graduated from Stanford, and I couldn't afford to get to New York or live in New York, so I came to Los Angeles. I got a job as a reader at ICM. At that time, they didn't have any readers so I was in a little tiny closet of a room.

It didn't really stick with me, but I remember that I loved reading scripts, distilling a story down to its essence. You're sitting in this dark room with no windows. You're in an agency, which is not the most creative environment, but somehow there was this lifeblood of movie people flowing through these scripts. I did that for about three months. It was interesting to me. I didn't know a lot about movies at the time.

I then moved to the *L.A. Times.* I had had an internship at the paper when I was in college, so Irv Letovsky, who was the editor at the time, said, "What are you doing being a reader at an agency? Come down here and get a real job."

So I went down there and got a "real job." And the job blossomed a bit. I began writing for the paper, and then I began writing about film.

Were you thinking of doing a novel like many journalists?

I had aspirations about writing a novel, but being a journalist is a full-time job, and I didn't have any illusions about doing it on the side. I had always wanted to do a novel but my writing got channeled into movies, I kind of lost the ability.

After three or four years at the paper, I got a little frustrated. I had gone to high school in Minneapolis and I knew Joel and Ethan Coen. We lived in the same neighborhood. Their first movie, *Blood Simple,* came out when I was at the *Times*. It had been a while since I took much pride in anything I was writing. Newspaper work is hard, a lot of day-to-day stuff. I remember thinking, if I interview Joel and Ethan I could write a profile that will remind people that I am a good writer because I had a subject that was worth writing about.

They were a great interview. They would finish each other's sentences, they were wildly creative, and they were from the Midwest. No one knew about them at that point. The story turned out well, and it wound up getting a great play in the *Calendar* section, with a great picture of Joel and Ethan looking out over the nighttime skyline of Los Angeles from the deck of Sam Raimi's house.

My getting into the movie business happened rather bizarrely. Don Simpson read that story in the morning paper. He had just lost his senior executive, Casey Silver. He said, "I've got to replace Casey, but I'm not going to go with any of the usual candidates in the business, I'm going to find someone outside the business—I'm going to hire this guy, who wrote the story in the *Times*."

Don Simpson was not the sort of personality that you say "no" to.

True, but I said "no" to him initially because going into the film business was such a foreign concept to me. He had some people follow up with me on his behalf and explain how rare the opportunity to work with Don and Jerry really was. But I still felt like the movie business was a totally alien world to me. I think I was the only person in movie history who refused to take a two-year contract and negotiated it down to one year because I was so sure I wouldn't fit into this world.

I had a great time with them. Don became a real mentor, and taught me a lot. They were inspiring to work for. Don was crazy. That's no secret, but they were making movies, and they were making movies that they loved. What I learned from that experience was that—Jerry does this to this day, and Don did this to his death—is that they work on things that they are truly passionate about.

Don wrote me a note when I left. I still have it, and it says you should always know what your point of view is. Know what you feel, know what you think, and always operate from that. Don't operate politically. Don never acted politically, often to his great detriment.

I got offered a studio job through Stacey Snider, whom I had hired as my assistant at Simpson-Bruckheimer. Stacey moved on but recommended me to Roger Birnbaum, who had just taken over production at Fox. I was v.p. of production, then senior v.p. of production, on and on. It was a good job in that I learned a lot about the studio world, the financing work, the distribution world, the marketing world—it was a very smart group of people at the time. Joe Roth was running Fox. Tom Sherak was running distribution. Those were mentor figures for me.

As time went by, there were management changes, and I began to feel that I wasn't in the right place. I began to feel that I was really far from what I really wanted to do. I went to Peter Chernin and said, "I want to stay here but I can't be an executive any more. Something is not working for me here, and you're not going to get my best work." So I became a producer at the studio. But what was frustrating to me was that I was still at the studio. I was making movies that they wanted to make. So I left. The deal expired, and I went home without an assistant.

You were going to do it "cold turkey." It must have been daunting.

It was back to my roots as a journalist: "What can you do on your own?" Me and the typewriter. I wanted to do the thing which scared me the most, which has always been a good guide for me. If something is really scary, there is a reason it is really scary, and you just shut your eyes and do it. So I did it, and it was hard at the time. But I began to attract a little group of projects that interested me. I met Catherine Hardwicke who had just written the script *Thirteen*. A friend of mine, Rex Pickett, had written a novel *Sideways*. From that nucleus of projects, I began to feel that I was doing something that I loved again. I wasn't yet producing them. I was just finding them.

Well, that's the trick, finding them. Finding a kindred sensibility.

Exactly, being true to your identity, having a point of view, as Don said. I think when I was working at Fox I didn't have a point of view.

You just try to second-guess the corporation?

Yes, and "How do I survive in this environment?" So with that process of finding things that I loved, I began to get excited about the people I was working with. Catherine was really inspiring for me to work with on *Thirteen*.

I reviewed that for **The Hollywood Reporter** *at Sundance. I still remember seeing it in the Library and seeing your credit. At the time I didn't know you were producing.*

It was my first movie. It really was an important moment to me. It still may be the most exciting moment I've had in the movie business, that screening in the Library at Sundance. I remember making the movie and thinking that nobody would ever see it, much less distribute it.

Then we went to Sundance, went with Nikki Reed and Evan Rachel Wood. It was sort of half-documentary and half-feature, and we had that screening. As the credits rolled, my cell phone began to buzz. I remember Peter Rice of Fox Searchlight was the first name that flashed up on the screen. He was in the back of the theater. And a lot of people that I knew, their names were showing up on my cell. That was a real great feeling. We had one of those all-night bidding situations. That gave me great confidence to do only things that I wanted to, that I felt passionate about. *Sideways* came out of that, and *The Illusionist*, and *The Family Stone*.

Those were more mainstream.

They weren't any less special to me. So, out of that, I guess I kind of forged a new identity, and said, "What kind of a producer do I want to be? And what does a producer like that really do?"

At that point I felt that a producer was someone who finds the material, and I knew what happened when you got to the studio, but everything in between was a mystery to me. I hadn't gone to film school, hadn't worked my way up through production. So what I got to do with all those movies was learn. I learned around some really extraordinary directors. And they were all, except for *The Illusionist*, movies where I was the only producer. I also made a movie called *Forty Days and Forty Nights*, a commercial comedy that had a very unique voice. The director was Michael Lehman, whom I had become close to during my years at Fox, where he made the comedy *Airheads.*

When I was doing these movies, there wasn't a giant producing team, which there often is on movies now. It was just sort of me with these scripts and filmmakers. It was a great learning experience to be responsible and to learn. All of those movies were made by teams of people who were just motivated by making a great movie. *Sideways* was kind of the peak of that, having the confidence that you could make something that everyone in the world would want to see.

During those first few years I was just kind of like ... "*Whatever.*" I was reading, grabbing onto things. I miss that feeling a lot. I'm not sure the movie business affords people the opportunity to do that any more. It is much more difficult to get movies made that are a little bit offbeat. Then you become part of the system that you were outside. Still, you try to do that in a way that you don't lose your sense of identity. Sometimes you just need to get movies made. You have a family, you have kids, and you want to be productive. Being a producer is a twofold job. First, you have to have the picture in your head at every moment more vividly than anyone else. Secondly you must function on a micro level, or a mundane level. You have to connect the big picture with all these little everyday choices about wardrobe, editing, production design. There are people who are very good at the day-to-day, and there are people who are very good about the big picture. What I aspire to be, and I don't think I've succeeded entirely, is to be able to try to do both.

As I made movies, I drew a lot on the time I had spent at Simpson-Bruckheimer. I didn't have the skill set to be the kind of producer who's on the set attending to every detail like Jerry Bruckheimer. Don was a brilliant conceptual thinker, but he wasn't necessarily around when the movie was getting made because he didn't have the attention span for it. I tried hard to have a bit of both of them in me, which was Jerry's eye for detail and Don's expansiveness.

You founded your own production company, Groundswell, in 2005.

There was money available then for producers like myself to form companies like Groundswell. I worked with Goldman-Sachs. I went to New York and was able to raise the funds. We made ten movies at

Groundswell. We continue to make movies as Groundswell, but we don't have the fund any more. With Groundswell my role shifted into being a different kind of producer. That was interesting, but it was hard. I wasn't the producer who was there every day. I was working with other producers on simultaneous projects. I was also responsible for the financial relationship with the investors.

What you knew about financing came from being an executive at Fox?

I didn't really have any financing expertise. I just tried to consult with good people. My first movies were really a baptism by fire because I don't really have a natural aptitude for the business side of things. In order to be a financing producer, I had to learn a tremendous amount about something that was more alien to me. It was different from working at a studio because at a studio you never feel that you're on the line. When you raise money, you really know the investors, you know them personally. You want to make them money. Now I have a real conscientiousness as a producer.

I used to say when I was producing that I can't worry about whether a movie is going to make money. I just have to worry about making a good movie. I think that was a little too clever and cavalier. I realized as I became a financing producer that the producer's job is to make the best movie possible, but you also have to be responsible that a movie has a sound financial basis. In the current world where money is very scarce for movies, the investment has to be protected. That's a primary concern for me now.

Possibly your naïveté helped you?

Maybe the movies made more money because of that, who knows? Now I always have that other side of my head saying, "Is this a smart investment? Does this make sense? Or should it be done differently?" I didn't worry about that as much early on in my career. It is a much more difficult now because money is so scarce in the independent world. Plus, the studios are not making character-driven movies.

All special effects, superheroes, aliens or vampires...

I can't really throw myself into producing those movies, even if they wanted me, which I am not sure they would. I think the days of being a producer just driven by passion are tough. You also have to be financially responsible, and movies have to be made for less money than they have ever been made for before because you're competing with television. Movies have to have a real reason for audiences to come. All of a sudden you have to have all these different equations in your head that were not necessary five years ago.

I was glad when I learned you were working with Tom McCarthy for **The Visitor.** *I loved* **The Station Agent,** *again, a movie about people, a human story.*

Well, that goes back to that thing that Don taught me: "Don't try to figure out what anyone else wants to see, just figure out what you want to see." In Don and Jerry's case, it was mainstream movies. Jerry loves the movies that he makes, and it shows. Different people have different tastes, but the lesson to be learned is: Be true to what you love. If all else fails, at least you'll get some personal satisfaction, and you'll probably connect with other people too. If you're sitting around trying to figure out what is going to work, what other people are going to like, you're always going to be behind. You're never going to be ahead of what people want to see.

You produced a nice range of movies at Groundswell.

When you go from making one movie a year to two or three a year, you have to move sideways a bit. And there are a lot of genres that interest me besides just independent drama. I love comedy, and I like things that are scary and intense. I like science fiction. I just want them to have characters I care about. For me it's less about genre than about being distinctive in any genre you are in. Do a horror movie, but how do you find a way into it that I care about and that are specific to their world? There are horror movies that I've watched that meant a lot to me. There are kids' movies I've watched that have meant a lot to me. I don't imagine working in the animated world, but when I saw *Up*, I thought, "Wow. That is a real work of art."

As you've been around longer as a producer, more material comes to you so it's a little easier to find. You have more confidence too. That has allowed a little more volume, but I still try to make it so that everything feels personal. Sometimes it's hard. I can get spread too thin.

What about when you release the film? It's out of your control.
That is becoming more and more of the job. How do you get a film to reach audiences in a fragmented world? It used to be the studios made the ads, and the producer waited for the Friday night grosses. You have to be much more involved now. There's social media and many more advertising platforms. There's more uncertainty and surprises.

Your background in writing carries over to your movies. The writer part of you is always there.
The primary vision of a film is from the director or the writer-director. Yet a producer who can meaningfully help a writer-director do their best work is really important. There's a great gulf between many filmmakers and their best work and their lesser work. I think a producer's job is to help them develop their vision more completely, and often that means being a real creative partner to them: pushing them, definitely engaging with them. Not just being critical, but collaborative.

I do work hard, and I don't think that's just at the script stage. If a performance does not feel true to what I imagined, it's really helpful to be able to discuss that with a director. A good director will listen and say "You're right" or "You're wrong." Or "You're partially right." I've been lucky to work with directors who were not threatened with that kind of partnership.

Alexander Payne was really influential to me on that. He would listen to an idea from anyone, and 99 percent of the time he would say, "I disagree with you." But he listened, and he listened thoughtfully, and he welcomed dialogue. He thrives on ideas. That was really fun. For me, being a producer at its essence is that partnership—that you have a creative voice in what you're doing. It's not just project-oriented or managing the pieces of it.

LONDON'S FILMOGRAPHY

Producer

Let It Snow (2015)
Trumbo (2015)
The Final Girls (2015)
Nightlight (2014)
Very Good Girls (2013)
Lola Versus (2012)
Win Win (2011)
All Good Things (2010)
Smart People (2008)
The Mysteries of Pittsburgh (2008)
The Visitor (2008)

King of California (2007)
The Illusionist (2006)
The Family Stone (2006)
Sideways (2004)
House of Sand and Fog (2003)
Thirteen (2003)

Executive Producer

The Hollars (2015)
The Informant! (2009)
Milk (2008)
Appaloosa (2008)

Fred Roos

Fred Roos is highly regarded as a creative producer who works in harmony with major filmmakers. He has had long-time associations with such filmmakers as Francis Ford Coppola and George Lucas.

A legendary casting director before he began producing, Roos has cast numerous noteworthy films, including Petulia, Zabriskie Point, Five Easy Pieces, The Godfather, The Black Stallion *and* Fat City. *He is credited with furthering the early careers of Harrison Ford, Teri Garr, Jack Nicholson, Kris Kristofferson, John Cassel and Frederic Forrest. He also gave movie audiences their first significant looks at such future stars as Diane Lane, Tom Cruise, Richard Dreyfuss, Laurence Fishburne, Rob Lowe, Matt Dillon, Patrick Swayze and Emilio Estevez.*

Roos segued from casting into producing under Coppola's aegis in 1973. (He had worked first with Coppola as a casting director for The Godfather.*) He went on to serve as co-producer of* The Conversation *and* The Godfather: Part II.

Roos' producing credits include such well-regarded films as New York Stories *(the "Life Without Zoe" segment),* Tucker, Barfly, The Secret Garden, Drive, He Said, *and* St. Vincent.

When Coppola purchased Hollywood General Studios in the early 1980s to serve as the L.A. base of his Zoetrope Studios, Roos became part of the management team. During the Zoetrope period he co-produced Hammett, The Escape Artist, The Black Stallion Returns *and* One from the Heart. *He found* The Outsiders *and nurtured the work after reading a letter sent to Coppola by an elementary school in Fresno "nominating" him to make a movie from the S.E. Hinton novel.*

He executive-produced and appeared in Hearts of Darkness: A Filmmaker's Apocalypse, *a documentary of the calamities plaguing the troubled jungle shoot. Roos received a CableACE Award and an Emmy Award nomination for his role as its executive producer. For Coppola,*

Roos also served as special consultant on Peggy Sue Got Married *and was co-executive producer on* Gardens of Stone.

A native of Southern California, Roos attended UCLA with a major in theater arts–motion pictures. After graduation, he traveled through Europe and then was drafted. During his Army service, Roos directed orientation documentaries in Korea for the Armed Forces Radio and Television Network.

Upon his discharge, Roos began his entertainment career in the mail room of the MCA agency, where he rose to agent. He subsequently served as a story editor and casting director for Robert Lippert Productions, a low-budget company for which he produced two Jack Nicholson action movies in the Philippines, Back Door to Hell *and* Flight to Fury. *He later was associate producer for Nicholson's first directorial effort,* Drive, He Said. *During his early career Roos also cast episodes of* The Andy Griffith Show *and* Mayberry R.F.D., *and 112 episodes of* That Girl.

More recently, he served as executive producer on a number of indie films for Francis Ford Coppola, including Youth Without Youth, Tetro *and* Twixt. *He also served as executive producer on the Sofia Coppola films* Lost in Translation, Marie Antoinette, Somewhere *and* The Bling Ring, *as well as serving as co-producer of* The Virgin Suicides.

Duane Byrge: When you were in film school in the '60s you had already decided to be a producer.

Fred Roos: I think I was the only guy in film school at UCLA who wanted to be a producer. I didn't voice that. It was kind of a cliché that producers were cigar-smoking, chain-wearing bad guys. Everybody wanted to be a writer, director or editor. They wanted to make documentaries. I studied all that, and I knew it was not my skill. I knew how to put things together. I knew how to recognize talent. I knew how to bring different talents together. I could write, and I directed my student film, but I knew that I didn't meet my standards. I had my own standards, and in these areas I didn't meet my standards as a writer or a director. I didn't want to just be something ordinary.

You brought acting talent together on TV with such programs as The Andy Griffith Show.

I could put all the quirky talents together. Mike Fenton and I were partners in casting in the '60s. I cast *Andy Griffith, That Girl, I Spy*. I always liked being around actors and actresses. Those types of people are never boring. I love being around great talent, great directors.

You have a reputation as someone who gets along with every-one, a diverse range of people and personalities.

I can't think of a single filmmaker that I didn't get along with. I got along great with Richard Lester, for whom I cast *Petulia*. When I would go to England we would visit. *Petulia* was shot in 1967, and we shot entirely in San Francisco. It was Haight-Ashbury. I was right in the middle of this. You don't realize what you're in when you're in it. I saw the Grateful Dead, Janis Joplin and a lot of great musicians. There was an improv group there called The Committee. I got all those per-formers parts in movies. It was great to be in San Francisco at that time.

Talk about your bap-tism into being a producer.

I had been working at this company, Robert Lip-pert's company. I was head of casting, I was assistant story editor—I was, basi-cally, an assistant to every-body. Jack Nicholson and Monte Hellman were in my private circle of friends. They were my people I ran around with. I put together these two films with Monte and Jack and got Lippert to finance them. He allotted no more than $100,000 each. So I was a kid and was brought into a foreign coun-try, the Philippines, to make these films on that budget.

Fred Roos, c. 2015. Courtesy Fred Roos Productions.

We had to crew-out locally. Monte was the director, but the head of the crew was Filipino. I recruited the crew, along with Monte. It was quite an undertaking. I ended up being in the Philippines a year. I rented a house with multiple bedrooms and bathrooms, and in-house keepers. We all lived there together, Monte, Jack, I and the other actors. It was quite exciting.

I'd like to buy the story rights to that. There must have been some real adventures.

Oh, God. [*Long pause*] I had a Filipino editor come at me with a knife.

He didn't agree with your suggestions?

FR: I kept bugging him: "Where's the film?" He was protecting it for some reason—more money, maybe. I guess I was badgering him too much, and he came at me. He just flipped. Somebody jumped in and stopped him before he could get to me. That was a one-time thing. I loved working there and the people there. My experiences there on those low-budget films led me to lead Francis and everybody back there much later for *Apocalypse Now*. I still knew a lot of people there from those two low-budget movies.

Any knife attacks or near-death experiences on **Apocalypse Now?**

I thought I was going to die in a helicopter during a typhoon. You couldn't drive to Manila, so the helicopter took Francis, his wife Eleanor and me there. We were coming by the coast, right off the downtown of Manila. We could see there were ships crashed on the beach. And the helicopter was no higher than the buildings on our left. I feared that we were going to slam into the buildings. I was certainly happy to get to the ground.

You've worked with such a wide range of filmmakers, beginning in your casting days.

I worked with Claude Lelouch. I would be the one they would call on when they came to the States to make a movie. In reality, I was, perhaps, the only casting director who knew backwards and forwards their work. Somehow the foreign directors would always ask for me when they came here.

I was always a big admirer of Michelangelo Antonioni. He was a very austere, quiet man, and I got along with him famously when I worked with him early in my casting career. Years later, when he came back to make his last film, he had a stroke and couldn't speak. He asked for me then. I was beyond casting then. I had been a producer for many years. He asked me to work with him again. I couldn't refuse him, and I worked with him for many weeks on a movie that never got made. I helped him with casting.

Your casting eye is always on.

I love talking to actors. I don't like to do readings unless it's absolutely necessary. I am not a big believer in that process. I love actors who've studied and sacrificed and done theater. They've struggled. I try to meet actors. My door is always open. I could fill my whole day doing that, but I can't. When I'm in a restaurant or something, and the waiter or waitress is obviously a struggling actress or actor, I will sometimes talk to them, and maybe arrange to meet them properly at my office at a later time. They're often surprised when I tell them that I'm a producer.

I believe in an in-depth chat as opposed to a reading, which doesn't always tell you things. I remember the first time I met Bobby De Niro. He just could not get a real conversation going. He was bright, nice, with no attitude. It was just not his thing to be chatty. Years later when we were casting *Godfather II*, Francis and I knew him, and didn't want to bring him in for a formal interview. So we just took him to dinner one night. He did not realize that this was his audition. Through the course of a two-hour dinner, we decided he could pass for the young Vito Corleone. So we cast him in that role.

When we were casting *Godfather II* there were a lot of interesting and challenging things that happened. Al Pacino had been cast in *The Gang That Couldn't Shoot Straight*. We had wanted him for Michael Corleone. MGM would not let us have him. Finally, we had to get him out of *The Gang That Couldn't Shoot Straight*. There was a lawyer who was known as a mob lawyer. I don't remember his name. [Producer Robert] Evans knew him really well. Evans called the lawyer, so the lawyer called [president of MGM] Kirk Kerkorian and told him, "You are building two hotels in Las Vegas. I think you might have some labor problems if you don't release Al Pacino from his contract."

That's so fitting for a **Godfather** *movie: Making an offer that he can't refuse.*

That's the way I heard it, but I can't say for sure if it's true. So we got Pacino back, as we had wanted. Bobby got that part in *The Gang That Couldn't Shoot Straight.* He said he loved the little part of the young Vito Corleone in *Godfather II*, but he couldn't pass up the lead in *The Gang That Couldn't Shoot Straight.*

Did you ever tell him later that the dinner was his audition?

I don't think so. We cast another part that way in *Godfather II*, for the character of the old Jewish Mafiosi who was based on Meyer Lansky. We called him Hyman Roth in the movie. Francis and I had the idea to get Elia Kazan to play that part. We both wanted Kazan. He had an office right on Broadway where he did his writing. It was the crappiest little office. No air conditioning and the heat of a New York August. He was there in his writing mode, with his shirt off. It was a nice conversation and all that, but he ultimately turned down the role.

We next decided to try Lee Strasberg. You just don't invite someone of his stature, who had run the Actors Studio, in for an audition. We concocted this whole scam to look him over. We got Sally Kirkland to help us. She was a member of the Actors Studio, so I asked her to throw a party with a lot of people and invite Lee. So she threw a party, and there were about 100 people there. The whole purpose of the party was for Francis and me to observe and watch Lee Strasberg. So we chatted with him to see if he would be a good Hyman Roth. After the party we discussed him and came to the conclusion that he would be good for the part. So we offered it to him. I don't think Lee ever knew our real intention in having that party.

His kind of awkward acting style worked for the role. It was close to coming off stilted, but it was perfect. You remember the scene where you see Hyman Roth in Miami. They're in a suburban home, and he's sitting in there watching a football game. It's hot, and he's doesn't have a shirt on. Francis got that idea of Hyman Roth with no shirt from the

Kazan meeting. It's an image that stuck in his mind: that hot August day in New York with Kazan sitting there with no shirt in front of his typewriter trying to write his novel. It's a great image, a man in his 70s or 80s watching a football game with no shirt on. I remember it was a USC game because I got the broadcast rights.

In the *Godfather* days and with *The Conversation* as well, a lot of those films were kind of studio films. It was not a mission of going out and chasing down money like it is these days. It was more at that time of watching the budget and explaining the progress to the executives.

My job was to calm things down during the shooting. That's something that every producer does. If someone was ranting or raving one day about something, I would handle it. Calm them down. They were afraid to approach Francis with these sorts of things, so I smoothed things over. It's just something that every producer does. Doing a studio movie then was a whole different process than it is today. Now being a producer is different. You've got to go and get the financing. On these personal movies that Francis does today, he finances them himself.

Can you talk about Lost in Translation? *Bill Murray was great in it.*

Lost in Translation all goes back to the fact that Sofia [Coppola] always had a great eye for fashion and design. As a teenager in high school, she interned with Karl Lagerfeld in Paris. She later created a fashion line of her own, primarily hip clothing for teenage girls. Her line became quite successful. Her biggest market was Japan. She made many trips to Japan for the line and encountered similar cultural-shock experiences that Bill Murray did in the movie. That's where the story for *Lost in Translation* came from, her experiences in Japan while promoting her fashions. She stayed at that very hotel that's in the film, and they would take her out on the town. *Lost in Translation* came out of her own stories and her own experiences.

How did financing come about?

It came from about four different sources, including a Japanese company and Pathe. On Sofia's films, I have not been involved in that sort of thing. She's managed by Bart Walker, whose specialty is finding money for these types of films. He's very good at it. He was partners with John Sloss in a company called Cinetic. They split up, and Bart Walker is back at ICM. He'll be doing the same thing for her there.

How about putting something together today ... what's the process?

Now you have to chase money, private money. You have to raise it through somebody who wants to be in the movie business. Thank God for them. I always hope that they do well, and make back their stake. Also there are these kinds of indie companies that are in the foreign sales game.

If you have a piece of material, a script, the first thing you do is go attach a director. You've got to do that before you cast, because a director does not want to be handed, "Here's your cast." So you attach a director, and then you have to attract some actors that will encourage financing. It's not a process that I like. It wears you out before you even get to make the movie. You have these meetings and lunches with people who just want to be in on it. I have had so many of these meetings. Often it just goes to nothing because some people just like to have these meetings so they feel like they are in the game. I just had one about a week ago, but you can't ignore them. You never know.

There's a film we just released last year, *St. Vincent*. It was with a writer-director, Ted Melfi, who is a very successful commercials director. He wrote a terrific script. It was for Peter Chernin's company with the financing coming from the Weinsteins. That cast was wonderful: Bill Murray, Melissa McCarthy, Naomi Watts, Chris O'Dowd, and Terrence Howard. There's a new kid in it who was terrific, Jaeden Lieberher.

It was very well received, and Bill Murray was great. What's next?

There's a new project that Francis is writing. It is a story about three generations of an Italian-American family. Francis and I are already into the casting process. We always have great fun doing these films. Again, producing today involves doing it yourself, getting everyone together. Producing is constant, and there are always changes. I still work ten-hour days.

ROOS' FILMOGRAPHY

Producer

The Congressman (2015)
St. Vincent (2014)
Master Class (2013)
The Story of Luke (2012)
Expired (2007)
The Young Black Stallion (2003)
Town & Country (2001)
Radioland Murders (1994)
The Secret Garden (1993)
Wait Until Spring, Bandini (1989)
New York Stories (producer of the segment "Life Without Zoe") (1989)
Tucker: The Man and His Dream (1988)
Barfly (1987)
Seven Minutes in Heaven (1985)
Rumble Fish (1983)
The Outsiders (1983)
The Black Stallion Returns (1983)
Hammett (1982)
One from the Heart (1982)
The Black Stallion (1979)

Back Door to Hell (1964)
Flight to Fury (1964)

Executive Producer

Silver Skies (2015)
No Stranger Than Love (2015)
The Bling Ring (2013)
Twixt (2011)
Somewhere (2010)
Tetro (2009)
Youth Without Youth (2007)
Marie Antoinette (2006)
Lost in Translation (2003)
Hearts of Darkness: A Filmmaker's Apocalypse (documentary, 1991)
Gardens of Stone (1987)
The Escape Artist (1982)

Co-Producer

The Virgin Suicides (1999)
The Godfather: Part III (1990)
The Cotton Club (1984)
Apocalypse Now (1979)
The Godfather: Part II (1974)
The Conversation (1974)

Paula Wagner

Paula Wagner currently helms Chestnut Ridge Productions, developing and producing film, television, theater and new media projects. She has worked in the top ranks of the entertainment industry as a talent agent, producer and studio executive.

Wagner began her career at Creative Artists Agency where she spent 15 years representing some of Hollywood's top actors, directors and writers. In 1993 she moved on to producing and launched Cruise/Wagner Productions with her former CAA client Tom Cruise. For more than a decade, C/W produced critically acclaimed films including Mission: Impossible and sequels, Without Limits, Shattered Glass, Narc, The Others, Vanilla Sky, Elizabethtown, The Last Samurai, Ask the Dust and Steven Spielberg's War of the Worlds, which Wagner executive-produced.

Wagner was co-owner and CEO of United Artists Entertainment from 2006 to 2008. During her tenure, UA released the Robert Redford political thriller Lions for Lambs and the World War II drama Valkyrie.

Most recently, Wagner is collaborating with Desen International Media on a China–U.S. co-production of Moon Flower of the Flying Tigers, an epic World War II romantic drama based on a true story.

Her Broadway producing credits include The Heiress starring Jessica Chastain and David Strathairn, Grace starring Paul Rudd and Michael Shannon and Terrence McNally's Tony-nominated Mothers and Sons.

Wagner received Premiere magazine's Women in Hollywood Icon Award in 2001. The following year she was featured in Bravo's Women on Top, a documentary which profiled exceptional women in entertainment. In 2004, she and Cruise were honored by Daily Variety as "Billion-Dollar Producers." That same year they received the UCLA/Producers Guild of America Vision Award. In 2006, Wagner received the Sherry Lansing award from the Big Brothers and Big Sisters Organization.

In 2008, Wagner was honored by the Costume Designers Guild with its Swarovski President's Award. In 2011, she earned the Chicago Film Festival's Renaissance Award and in 2012 she was honored at the Deauville American Film Festival.

In addition to being on the board of the PGA, Wagner is a member of AMPAS, the Broadway League and a former member of Actor's Equity and Screen Actors Guild. She serves on the boards of Film Forum in New York, the American Cinematheque and National Film Preservation Foundation and is a Lifetime Trustee of Carnegie Mellon University, where she received her degree and is an adjunct faculty member. She also serves on the board of Carnegie Mellon.

Duane Byrge: Talk about your background and how it all led to becoming a movie producer.

Paula Wagner: I have had a number of careers in this business. Mainly in movies and theater, and some television. I started acting when I was 13 years old at the Youngstown Playhouse, which had professional standards. I studied and learned every aspect of the theater in college at Carnegie Mellon University. While I was studying acting, I was directing, playwriting, watching films like crazy. I was falling in love with film. I was seeing Bergman, Fellini, some of Pasolini, de Sica. I was also watching the French *auteurs*: Alain Resnais, Francois Truffaut and Claude Chabrol. Just film, film, film.

I took a year off from college and went to the Neighborhood Playhouse in New York and studied with Sandy Meisner. I was so into it: representational acting versus the Method Approach. He was very specific about what great acting was: The technique was about authenticity of the moment. So I learned all of this and later it became a foundation for my taste and understanding of the films and the talent with whom I wanted to work.

Right after college I watched a lot of things being created in terms of landmark entertainment. I was in the Broadway production of *Lenny*. This was an event. I got to know the assistant director, who changed his life later on, and his name was Harvey Milk. I worked with all of these amazing people. I understudied a new play from a new playwright named Terrence McNally. I became very involved in the women's movement because I was raised by a liberated woman. I co-wrote a play, *Out of Our Father's House,* assembled the production and acted in it. Rosalynn Carter brought it to the White House. Later it was aired on PBS, and it's been presented in theaters worldwide.

I was an actress in the first mini-series, *Loose Change,* which was about the Mario Savio free speech movement at Berkeley, based on a book by Sara Davidson. I always kind of gravitated toward serious things. I did Broadway, I did Off Broadway. I played Maggie the Cat twice in *Cat on a Hot Tin Roof.*

I was part of that inner circle of the theater, but something was missing. I needed to actively create. I felt I needed more. I thought about directing because I had directed. I thought about writing. I thought about consulting. There were a lot of things that were kind of rolling around in my head. I didn't give up acting. I just needed other things.

You were heading toward being a producer, although you didn't know it.

Long story short, Susan Smith, who was my agent, offered me a job as an agent in 1978. It was that simple. Suddenly I went from being one of the young clients to being a young agent. I was delivering scripts to my friends who were the clients. I started doing it, and I realized that this was utilizing everything that I had done. It involved using everything from psychology to knowing how to read contracts. All of this was falling into place: "I've walked in these shoes." I knew how to talk to artists. I could talk to them about acting, their roles. When they would say, "I don't know how to do this character," I could help them. I could talk to people about the complexities of their performance and that just became a natural thing.

And, I was fearless. I was never afraid of being fired or taking risks. Don't be afraid, have a goal, set plans and follow your dream. That was my kind of thing. Life then takes you in other directions. Luck is something that doesn't just happen. You have to understand what luck is. People always say, "You have to have a little bit of luck." Well, to have luck, you have to be accessible and available to see an opportunity and seize it. I have always had this sense of daring. Although I'm a nice girl from Ohio, I'm kind of like, "What the hell, you go down this road once. I'm going to take a few risks."

So, now I was an agent, and I got a call from Fred Specktor at Creative Artists Agency: "We're looking for a lady agent." I'd heard about this agency: Mike Ovitz, Ron Meyer, and Bill Haber were the owners. They had terrific agents there, like Rick Nicita and Fred.

This was in 1980. I was intrigued, and thought, "Where is this little unknown company going to go?" but they sounded great to me. They had never recruited a female agent from outside of the company, but they had four or five women already there. I was the first one recruited from outside. I interviewed with Mike Ovitz and Ron Meyer and joined CAA. What did I know? I just knew I was going to be a great agent. I was pretty naïve, but I just believed in what I was going to do: I was going to sign talent and do a great job.

My first office at CAA was a converted Xerox room. Immediately I was assigned to handle TV talent and signing clients. Also, I had to cover studios. I was at the office on Christmas. I was going to work twice as hard and do what I had to do.

Being part of CAA at the time, we signed the talent, but we were also creating a model for an entertainment company. I was covering 20th Century Fox for CAA. Besides covering the studio, one of the goals I had was to discover talent and make movie stars. I was tenacious. I decided I was going to get to know every single person on the lot. I got to know the guard at the gate. I met Sherry Lansing. I met Dick and Lili Zanuck, David Brown, Stanley Jaffe, Les Moonves, Peter Chernin. I got to know all these people. Even though I was working with TV talent, I wanted to discover some new movie talent.

I got turned on to this

Paula Wagner, 1996. Courtesy Chestnut Ridge Prods.

movie *Taps*. I had known about it. They had done a long casting search because there was an actors' strike. I saw some dailies through my friend Richard Fischoff. I saw these two phenomenal actors, Sean Penn, and Tom Cruise, a young, undiscovered talent.

I co-signed Sean and signed Tom. I later signed Tim Hutton. I started working with young talent. My passion was taking young talent and finding the right movies for them. I loved the idea of packaging. I was at CAA for 13 years, and I placed Sean Penn in *Fast Times at Ridgemont High* and Tom Cruise in *Risky Business*. Then Matthew Broderick became a client of mine and I placed him in *Ferris Bueller's Day Off*.

It was the '80s and we were a part of the energy of what was happening then. It was an amazing time. We thought we were at the beginning of something. But as we moved into the '90s and the 2000s, I realized we were at the end of an era of filmmaking. Think about 2014 versus 1984. Think about the change. The whole business has gone through a massive revolution—we're still going through it. Nobody really knows absolutely where it is all going.

At CAA, in addition to working with young talent, I started signing and working with directors and writers such as Robert Towne and Oliver Stone. I packaged talent for *Born on the Fourth of July*. I saw myself as an advocate for talent. For me, being an agent was like a calling. It was a different time in the role of the agent. I was an agent and a manager, all rolled up into one. I put films together and realized I was now a producer.

I decided to form a production company. In 1993, Tom Cruise and I became business partners. He had this really uncanny ability to see the whole picture, and he was always interested in every detail of the film. I had worked with him since he was a young, unknown actor. So, I joined forces with Tom, and we started Cruise/Wagner Productions. John Goldwyn approached us about coming to Paramount. There I encountered Sherry Lansing and Stanley Jaffe, whom I had known from my days at Fox. I moved into this famous Hollywood office on the Paramount lot. It went all the way back to Joe Kennedy from the RKO days. It even had a dumbwaiter, where he used to bring Gloria Swanson up. Howard Hughes had been in that office, and Lucille Ball and Sherry when she was a producer.

Our first film for Cruise/Wagner was *Mission: Impossible*. It was a classic TV series that I loved as a kid. Paramount Pictures owned the rights. They had been trying to make a film of it for some time. Tom Cruise also loved it. After a number of meetings, Cruise/Wagner Productions came aboard *Mission: Impossible* to develop a film to star Tom Cruise. The original series dealt with the Cold War. We had to find a way to develop it so it had a team, yet Tom Cruise was the leader of the team. It needed to be post–Cold War. It had to be an international film. We were just on the threshold in '93 of the film industry entering the international marketplace in a major way.

It was not about movies just made for the United States any more. This was one of the things we were looking to do, to make it international with the plotlines and the casting. There was a very strong vision about this. We wanted something that had a lot of suspense. We wanted something with an amazing character for Tom Cruise, and we wanted something that had a lot of twists and turns that you never saw coming. We brought on great writers, including Steve Zaillian who worked on a treatment. Robert Towne and David Koepp ultimately wrote the final *Mission: Impossible.*

The goal was to make a stand-alone feature. We wanted to keep the theme song but re-invent it. We were looking to have a film that was suspenseful. This *Mission* had to be carried out over two hours of details leading up to the denouement of what this mission was about, and what it had accomplished. We wanted to have a major feature director. We brought in Brian de Palma as director, one of the masters of suspense. He had done a series of great films such as *Carrie* and all the way back to *Hi Mom* and *Greetings.* We began to work with him, and we carefully analyzed what the inspiration was for the series, *Mission: Impossible.* How was this fulfilled in the television series, and how could it be converted to a film?

As a producer, you often start with the germ of an idea that then has to be developed into a script. Script development is probably the most challenging aspect of making a film. The script has to become something that works on the screen, not just on the page. We had to create a character that worked for Tom Cruise. Tom is a great actor, and he had played some amazing roles—*Born on the Fourth of July, Rain Man, A Few Good Men.* We had to find a great character for him, one that put him in the center of the action and gave him a lot of challenges to overcome, an "impossible mission." The real challenge was finding that character.

Another goal of *Mission: Impossible* was to find a new international location for the film. We shot in Prague and London. It certainly was challenging. It took a substantial group of people working together. We had an American crew and based our film in the U.K. We worked with the local studios there. We had production entities in Prague. We were trying to speak the common language known as film.

Prague had just changed its whole governmental structure. We were really the first production company at a major studio to show contemporary Prague in a film. We used a number of locations, including a sequence on the Charles Bridge. One of the things about producing films internationally is that you not only have to have a firm grip and understanding of the various production requirements within the country, but you also have to have an understanding of the governmental and political structure of the country. As a film, you are bringing business into a country, but you also have to understand and respect the structure of the country.

We had the opportunity to meet with Vaclav Havel. Tom Cruise, Jon Voight and I had a meeting with him. He was not only a political leader, the first president of the post–Communist Czech Republic, but he was an artist, playwright and poet.

Another goal was to cast it internationally. Brian de Palma's thoughts were to bring in French actors, which we did—Emmanuelle Beart and Jean Reno. One of the things about being a producer is that you work closely with your director and your star. In that case, the star was also the producing partner. We worked to cast against type. Ving Rhames was chosen for a role as the genius computer geek. De Palma loved this idea and actually merged two characters into the Ving Rhames character. He was the computer genius and the sidekick of Tom Cruise. He was fantastic and was in every *Mission* movie thereafter.

Vanessa Redgrave's part was originally written for a man. She played the ultimate villain—the moral villain, the intellectual villain. There's a great scene where Tom is brought in wearing a hood and put in front of the real villain, and lo and behold, it's a woman—Vanessa Redgrave.

You also had Jon Voight in a bad-guy role, which was new for him.

Jon Voight was always known as a good guy. This was Brian de Palma's brilliance; to twist and turn what you think is real. You think something is real, but then in fact what you think is reality is not.

When it came to the soundtrack, we wanted to take the *Mission: Impossible* theme and re-invent it. We had numerous discussions and conversations. Our final idea was for Larry Mullen Jr. and Adam Clayton of U2 to reinvent the *Mission: Impossible* theme song with a very modern feel to it.

The other aspect of it was to have action sequences. We did two action sequences that you've never seen before. We came up with this idea—again, this is a tribute to Brian de Palma—this idea of going into a tunnel with a helicopter chasing a train where Tom Cruise is clinging to the top of the train. Visual effects were just beginning to be really authentic at that time. We worked with great visual effects artists like John Knoll of Industrial Light & Magic. He's now very renowned, but he was just starting then. ILM did things for this train sequence that had never been done before. Now it's commonplace, but when Tom Cruise was stretched out on top of the train, we had to have huge fans blowing on his hair to show motion on the train. It's very challenging to mix the visual effects with what is actually happening in the sequence.

How did you interface with the technical people?

Everybody was a pioneer. We were all learning. I remember conversations where someone would say, "How much does it cost to erase the wires on somebody?" There were no set rules. It was pioneering into the world of effects. There were a lot of firsts on *Mission: Impossible.*

This was the first film that I had produced. I learned a lot. This was where my background came into play. I felt like I had been doing this forever through my years as an agent, being involved with all my clients' films, and my years as an actress. Having done film work, having walked in the shoes, been on the set, I felt comfortable in this environment. I wasn't afraid to ask questions. I was open with the fact that it was my first film. I knew that I was bringing a certain breadth of experience and what I didn't know I would learn quickly.

Once we finished the film and did press for it, there was an attitude about "How could you take a TV series and turn it into a motion picture?" I said, "How come Shakespeare adapted *Plutarch's Lives* into his plays?" Whatever the source of the material, the important thing is what ends up on the screen.

Marketing is another aspect. Once you have the film finished, how do you market it? Where do you present the film? This was one of the first films that was presented internationally. It was a real credit to Tom Cruise that he traveled the world supporting the film. Everybody was in unknown territory. It was well received. It was a first in terms of an American-based film that was shot internationally with international cast members. It was presented as a big event.

This *Mission* was the beginning. I'm very proud of the fact that it has spawned a powerful franchise that has gone on and on, and will continue to go on. I'm proud to have been one of the original creators.

You have shot the series all over the world.

We shot *Mission II* in the United States and in Australia. We even had a section that was supposed to be shot in Spain, but we set it up in Australia. We cast Scottish actor Dougray Scott as the international villain. We had some wonderful Australian actors and again, Tom Cruise and Ving Rhames. We also had [director] John Woo, who was well known for having done a certain kind of film. His particular skill was his beautiful, ballet-like visual moves, the way he dealt with action. This was very action-oriented and also designed to be international. Robert Towne wrote the script. It had a love story in it, and a lot of the same elements as [the first *Mission: Impossible* movie]. Thandie Newton was cast as the love interest.

Once again, we re-invented the theme song. We had Limp Bizkit do that. We even had Metallica do a song for us. I believe *Mission: Impossible II* was the first film that was released internationally day-and-date because it had over the years built a huge international following. The whole span from the development of *Mission: Impossible* in 1993 to the completion and release of *Mission III* in 2006 was 13 years.

The third one was with J.J. Abrams in his film debut as a director. I had known him as a writer. He was a very talented screenwriter. We had seen the pilot of *Lost*, which he had just completed, but no one else had seen it. He did a wonderful job, and we convinced the studio—I have to say that Tom Cruise was passionate, and instrumental in convincing them that J.J. Abrams would make a brilliant *Mission: Impossible III* director. Sherry Lansing and the studio accepted that.

Mission: Impossible III was one of the greatest experiences I have had as a producer. At that point, I had produced many films, and I felt like I was really on my game. Producing a movie to me is both an art and a craft.

J.J. Abrams is a phenomenally collaborative artist. I felt a real rapport in working with him to help find the best crew. He brought people he trusted, and we brought people we trusted. We surrounded them with top technical people. We had various writers working on the script, like Alex Kurtzman, Roberto Orsi and J.J. Abrams. It was like a well-oiled machine. We worked very closely with China and the China Film Group for the sequence in Shanghai. Also, we wanted to be one of the 20 foreign films to be shown in that country, and we worked very hard to facilitate that.

We filmed a sequence in Italy, second units in Germany, Virginia and Shanghai. We were one of the first major studio films to film in China. That took a long time to set up. We had approvals of the script, of what it was we were going to shoot, and again, we had a centerpiece action scene for Tom Cruise. We had this amazing skyline in Shanghai where he jumps off of a skyscraper. He had wanted to do the real thing, but we ended up shooting some of the jump from a sound stage in L.A.

That would have given everyone a heart attack.

In *Mission: Impossible II* when Tom was hanging off the top of the mountain, that was real. John Woo said, "One take, cut. That's it." That was Tom Cruise really hanging, and it's not something that I encouraged.

You followed up the first Mission: Impossible *with* Without Limits. *I was pleasantly surprised at the time that C/W had gone from such a big film as* Mission *to a low-budget indie about a long-distance runner.*

I was Robert Towne's agent previously at CAA. When we were

doing *Mission*, we brought him on to work with us. He wrote this beautiful spec script about long-distance runner Steve Prefontaine. Tom and I were attracted to this project. We knew it wasn't a big movie, but it was so beautiful. It was so much about competing with yourself, reaching for something outside of yourself, reaching beyond where you might be in spite of the obstacles. I think every movie has to have "and the moral of the story is...." It's like a kid telling a story. Every movie has to have a center, a thematic that means something.

Steve Prefontaine was a maverick, a bit of a loner. He defined in a way the spirit of a generation. He was at the Munich Olympics when the Israeli athletes were killed. He ran in spite of it, but came in fourth, I think. It put him in a depression, but he was going to come back out and go at it again. And then he was killed in a car crash. Both Tom and I were attracted to this story. I think that it was admirable that a major movie star, such as Tom, supported this film. Terry Semel and Bob Daly at Warners showed great support for the project. This movie would not get made now at a studio. We shot it in Oregon on a low budget. We had real Olympic athletes in it, and we found new actors. We found this kid named Billy Crudup.

It was really exhilarating to be around Conrad Hall as he shot the movie. His dignity, his ferocity and artistry as a director of photography were mesmerizing. He was intense and determined about it: "We don't just do what television does with close-ups. We go big, we go wide, and we show the context of the world." That was fantastic.

Working with Robert Towne was great. He'd sit there and say, "Wait a minute, kid." He'd re-write stuff on the spot. And in the editing room was Dede Allen, one of the greatest editors ever. Through her cutting, she would create a story. She knew how to make performances work. I used to sit in the editing room with her, and I learned a lot from these sessions.

During this time, I saw a film called *Abre los ojos* [*Open Your Eyes*]. I sent it over to Tom, and he said it was phenomenal. We bought the film, and got Cameron Crowe to adapt it as *Vanilla Sky*. It was an unusual story set in Madrid. We worked very closely with the original director Alejandro Amenabar. We set it in New York City. The big challenge of this film was that there was one sequence where the actor in Spain ran wildly in his dream through the main street in Madrid. There was nobody there. It was one of those nightmarish moments where you run down the street and it's all deserted. We decided we were going to do that in Times Square, and the goal was to shut down Times Square and have Tom Cruise running through it.

We worked with the city of New York, with the film commission and with our various technical advisers to shut down Times Square. We couldn't rehearse in Times Square. We had to choreograph the scene on the top of a building. We had five hours, from 5 a.m. to 10 a.m. on a Sunday in October to shoot that sequence. We did some green-screen. I think there were a few people who straggled into the shot who had to be digitally erased. And we changed some of the billboards, of course. Other than that, it was a real sequence. You could never shut down Times Square now. That was a historic moment.

In the meantime, we came on board with *The Last Samurai.* This was an interesting film. It was a project that Ed Zwick and Marshall Herskowitz had worked on from John Logan's script. Tom came in to star and we also joined as producers. We had all known each other, and it was a very collaborative team. It was Ed Zwick and Marshall Herskowitz and Cruise/Wagner coming together to produce the film at Warner Bros. This film shot much of the time on the Warner Bros. lot. We had to create old Japan. We shot ten days in Japan, and the rest of it in New Zealand that had to look like late 19th-century Japan.

I can remember standing on this slushy field in the middle of the night in New Zealand. I had two cell phones in my hands. I was in my big boots. The Samurai were charging the Japanese army in this big battle scene. We would shoot one side of thousands of Samurai coming straight at you. When we got that, the Samurai players would run into tents, change their clothes and they would become the military. For the scene, we had a thousand Japanese extras who didn't speak English. We had the finest horse trainers, horsemen from Spain. We had a crew from Scotland, Ireland, and Italy. We had Chinese people, Japanese people—we were bringing the world together in the name of making a film. Now our visual effects were more sophisticated than before. We were doing visual effects where they would create the arrows that were flying through the air.

So I'm standing in this slushy battlefield, watching this major battle. It was exhilarating. My cell phone rings, and it's my son, and, "Mom, can you help me with my homework?" He's in L.A. Then another call comes in from another studio, and they say, "There's this script you turned in, and we all hate it. What do you want to do?" And a third call is coming in from L.A. about "What are you going to do with the fact that you may be running over and what are you going to do with the budget overages? How are you going to compensate for that?" Three calls coming. I, of course, took the call from my son first. I have never lost sight of that. For me, as taxing and exciting as all of this is, my family has always come first.

Logistically, it sounds overwhelming to produce and co-ordinate all of that.

That was a very physical production. The job of a producer shifts with every film, it changes. That's what is so fascinating about being a producer. The producer's role can change, but at the end of the day the producer is the one who has shepherded the project from the very beginning all the way to the last print or the last digital. And then you get involved with marketing and distribution. I've shot films in many different countries, and I've worked with various governments.

What does that entail?

Red tape, brokering deals. Through *Mission: Impossible*, we were always first. I would deal with crews. I worked with the Chinese cultural people to get the movie shot in China. We shot about three weeks there, and shot Prague, Australia, Italy, New Zealand, all over the place. So I'm pretty knowledgeable about international.

I've actually shot more films internationally than domestically. I loved all of that, and a lot of traveling. I'd bring my son with me and my husband, Rick Nicita, would join us, and we worked it all out.

I made a crazy little film in New Mexico in the late '90s called *Suspect Zero*. The plot was about this serial killer chasing another serial killer. It starred Aaron Eckhart and Ben Kingsley. The "good guy" had to chase the bad guy to Tijuana, and he was looking around for the bad guy, drinking vodka and watching a young woman seductively dancing around a donkey. It was a background scene. Remember, this is an R-rated but not violent film. It was more of a psychological thriller. We kept shooting this scene, and finally the donkey handler said, "I want

my donkey off the set. This is really inappropriate. This woman is dancing around like that, and it's not appropriate to have my donkey in this
shot." I had just flown in—I was wearing a cowboy hat and boots—I
had to kind of broker this thing with the donkey handler and the AD.
Later on, the scene was cut. The shot wasn't even used. So, I was going
from trying to keep a donkey handler happy and then simultaneously
working with very dignified, political people.

I once chased an actor around the set to comb his hair because I
couldn't find the hair stylist. I said, "We're doing a close-up and I see
the wig line." This was maybe before I knew exactly what a producer
was supposed to do. I maybe thought a producer was supposed to do
anything that was not being done.

When you've produced more than one movie, sometimes they
work and sometimes they don't. Not everything is successful. I've made
movies that have not been successful. I've made mistakes too. When
we were leaving Paramount around 2006, a new regime came in. Then
the United Artists opportunity came along.

**Going in to revive the studio started by Charlie Chaplin, Doug-
las Fairbanks, Mary Pickford ... that must have been daunting?**
I was always fascinated with United Artists, with the artists having
control over their destiny. My vision was to respect and revere what
United Artists originally was: their great Academy Award-winning classic movies, their reverence for independent filmmakers, and the interesting, powerful films they produced. It was for us to bring UA into
the future. It takes a couple of years to really launch a company. Everything had to boot up right away. Our first film, *Lions for Lambs*, came
out with Robert Redford, Meryl Streep and Tom Cruise. Then we made
a film called *Valkyrie*, a great story about these people who sacrificed
their lives to end Hitler's reign. Chris McQuarrie wrote it. Tom was
terrific in it. I spent two years at UA, and I'm proud of the movies I
made.

You're the phoenix too, both pioneer and phoenix.
I started my own company, Chestnut Ridge, and I felt this incredible freedom. At that point I had done so much in my career: I was an
actress, I was an agent, I was a producer, and I ran a studio for two

years. "All I'm going to do now is from the heart," I said. "What do I love? I love the theater." While domestic film revenues are flat, live entertainment is growing. The potential is huge. Statistically, you are seeing the theater attendance rising on Broadway; however, the film industry has just seen its worst box office in eight years.

Everything in the industry changed in '08. The studios expanded, and now they're contracting. It's mostly tent poles and occasional romantic comedies. Now the demographics of the opening weekend are more internationally based. You can't have Robert Towne's beautiful language; the dialogue has to translate to all the cultures, so it's better to utilize imagery. We've made so many strides technologically. The film industry is business-dominant, creative-dominant or technology-dominant, and currently technology is the dominant force in filmmaking. Creativity now comes from the technology, not necessarily from the stories. The stories are pretty formulaic, basic.

I thought theater—that's unfinished business for me. I love the theater. I started reading all of my old plays. The first thing I did was *The Heiress* with Jessica Chastain, and then I did *Grace* with Michael Shannon. More recently I've come all the way back around with Terrence McNally's play *Mothers and Sons*. It was about the reorganization of family. I'm very proud of it and it was even nominated for a Tony.

You're now doing a movie co-production in China, Flying Tigers.

The Chinese company reached out to me to see if I would be interested in this story. They did it through CAA, which has a branch in China. I had already made a movie in China, and I really enjoyed that experience. I loved this story. It's a love story set during World War II involving a Chinese nurse and an American fighter pilot.

You've got a lot on your plate. How do you balance it all?

Lately I have been spending so much time in New York, and China, and I just came back from Europe. I'm producing *Pretty Woman* for Broadway.

My family is most important to me: My son Zach, my stepson Jesse and his wife Lizzie, my sisters and entire family, and my husband Rick Nicita. We've been married for over 30 years. I've learned to balance things; my family is more important than anything I've ever done in my career.

Wagner's Filmography

Producer
Jack Reacher (2012)
Death Race (2008)
The Eye (2008)
Mission: Impossible III (2006)
Ask the Dusk (2006)
Elizabethtown (2005)
Suspect Zero (2004)
The Last Samurai (2003)
Hitting It Hard (documentary short) (2002)

Vanilla Sky (2001)
Mission: Impossible II (2000)
Without Limits (1998)
Mission: Impossible (1996)

Executive Producer
War of the Worlds (2005)
Shattered Glass (2003)
Narc (2002)
The Others (2001)

Jim Wilson

He keeps a low profile, but Jim Wilson has been the quiet force behind an impressive array of films, from Oscar winners to blockbusters to small indies. Wilson and Kevin Costner partnered to form Tig Productions in 1988. Tig's 1990 epic Dances with Wolves *won seven Academy Awards, including Best Picture. In all, it received 12 nominations. Wilson and Costner also won the prestigious Golden Laurel Award from the Producers Guild.*

They sold Dances with Wolves *overseas first, pre-selling it to individual countries and territories, which raised a portion of the budget. Tig employed the same strategy financing future projects: They would launch the production with a foreign partner and secure a domestic distribution deal later.*

After their Dances with Wolves *triumph, Tig produced the romantic thriller* The Bodyguard, *which starred Costner and Whitney Houston and was written by Lawrence Kasdan. With Houston's shimmery, sensuous vocals bolstering the storyline,* The Bodyguard *became a blockbuster movie and musical mega-hit.*

Tig teamed with Kasdan again for Wyatt Earp *with Kasdan directing and starring Costner, Dennis Quaid and Gene Hackman. Costner and Wilson served as executive producers on the eight-hour TV documentary* 500 Nations, *the story of the American Indians' history from the earliest signs of man to the beginning of the 20th century.*

Wilson's interest in film began early. He made his first short film on Super 8 in high school. A star tennis player, he began shooting footage of his college matches and was encouraged by his tennis coach Jim McManus to continue shooting. He obtained a degree in film from the Berkeley Film Institute in 1979.

After competing on the pro tennis circuit, he devoted himself fulltime to capturing major tennis tournaments on film, including Wimbledon and the Davis Cup. He formed his own company, American Twist, producing and directing numerous short films and promotionals for Volvo, Kodak, World Team Tennis, Transamerica and the U.S. Tennis Association.

Wilson's dream was to direct. His first directorial effort in feature films was Stacy's Knights *(1983). It was written by Michael Blake, based on Wilson's story idea about an ordinary woman who does something extraordinary. (Blake went on to write the novel and script for* Dances with Wolves.*)* Stacy's Knights *starred newcomer Kevin Costner as a charismatic drifter; the relationship jelled between the actor and director. Shot on a very low budget,* Stacy's Knights *was completed in five weeks in Reno, Nevada. After they went their separate ways: Costner's star rose in a number of productions, while Wilson honed his skills producing and directing a mix of projects.*

Prior to forming Tig with Costner, Wilson produced Laughing Horse *in 1984 and directed* The Movie Maker *in 1986. He first worked on a studio film as associate producer of* Revenge, *which also starred Costner.*

More recently, Wilson directed Head Above Water, *a comedic thriller starring Harvey Keitel, Cameron Diaz and Craig Sheffer, and* Laffit: All About Winning, *a documentary about jockey Laffit Parcay Jr. He also directed the coming-of-age romance* Whirlygirl *starring Monet Mazur and Julian Morris. In 2013 Wilson produced and directed* 50 to 1, *an uplifting underdog story of Mine That Bird, a Kentucky Derby long shot.*

Tig's more recent productions starring Costner include the Capraesque Swing Vote *in which Costner plays a rube thrust into the political limelight when the presidential election comes down to his vote. In a tonal departure for the Wilson-Costner team,* Mr. Brooks *explored darker territory, with Costner playing a sociopathic family man/killer.*

Duane Byrge: How did you get started?

Jim Wilson: I was playing tennis for UC Berkeley, and I loved making small movie projects with friends. My tennis coach knew that I liked making movies. I guess you could say he was responsible for giving me my start. He asked me if I was interested in filming a tennis tournament, kind of like doing a highlight reel of the event. I had never done it, and I was enthused.

The first event was a Volvo-sponsored event in New Hampshire in the White Mountains. I think it was 1977. I went out and bought a 16mm camera and chose a few lenses. He let me buy what I needed, so I purchased a good zoom. I flew off with camera in hand. I had longer hair, and they would put me in the frisk department. I was a one-man band. I went and shot away for a week. Each tournament was a week long. As I shot away, I started to learn. I had a very limited budget. It was $12,000 for a half-hour show—that's small.

I was a one-man band from 1977 to '81. It was the school of hard knocks. I still pull from that today. Someone says, "You can't get that shot" or "I'm not sure that's viable," I tell them it is.

I started a company called American Twist. So I learned the producing, the necessity of keeping to a tight budget, and I was loading film in the dark. I was operating with everything and dealing with the labs as well. It just snowballed. I traveled for four and a half years, nonstop. I was doing over-the-shoulder interviews with Jimmy Connors, Bjorn Borg and John McEnroe—all the greats. I was in Argentina, Chile, England, Austria, Australia, all over the world. I was filming the big stuff: Davis Cup. Wimbledon, U.S. Open. It all came from playing college tennis and a guy saying, "Why don't you take a shot?"

You are a filmmaker who became a producer.

I actually started off wanting desperately to direct. I've directed half a dozen movies, beginning with *Stacy's Knights.* In trying to get *Stacy's Knights* launched, I realized I'd probably have to do it myself. So I got pretty good at raising money. I never felt embarrassed to ask for money. I always felt the arts were underfunded to begin with. It doesn't bother me. I've never done it in a corporate sense, but in terms of going to wealthy individuals, deep-pocketed folks and do a little bit of a dog-and-pony show, I didn't have a problem. I started off with friends of family.

We did [*Stacy's Knights*] for about a quarter million dollars. It was not a great film, but at the end of the day, Kevin saw very clearly that I could put a lot on the screen and make a lot of deals. Kevin saw what I could do in terms of producing. He remembered that. The five years after *Stacy's Knights*, I did pretty much what everyone else does in town. I directed some small films. I hustled. I'd write stuff. I did music videos, whatever was needed to pay the rent. Everything taught me a lot. I did a film on the greatest roller coasters in America. I did floral videos for Kodak. I did everything I could to stay alive.

Kevin and I remained friends. We would hunt and fish together during those five or six years, and I'd read scripts. He was catching fire—*Bull Durham, No Way Out.* He did his piece in *The Big Chill,* which got cut. He had three or four pretty damn good movies. We became fast friends. So we formed Tig in 1988, and the two of us would look at material.

Where did you get "Tig"?

Tig is Kevin's grandmother's nickname. His family is from Gyman, Oklahoma. When he told me he wanted to call it Tig, I was skeptical. I told him that "Tig" kind of sounds like it stands for some conglomerate, transcontinental something-or-other. But, it was named for a very independent grandma. I never loved the name, but it was never changed. We never did have a contract between us, it was all on a handshake. That's what it's always been. Obviously, the majority of the mate-

Jim Wilson on the set of *50 to 1* (2014) at Churchill Downs. Courtesy Jim Wilson.

rial we received was for him to star in. We both talked about directing material, but we knew that he would take the forefront because he had the cachet. We knew what each other did very well, and Kevin always played his part beautifully. It was a great relationship. We made a lot of films together.

Dances with Wolves *was one of the most daunting and unlikely productions ever made.*

Dances started with a friend of mine, Michael Blake. I met Michael at Berkeley. He was actually driving a bus. I was going from one class to another, and he was the driver. We met up literally on the bus at Berkeley. We found out that we were going to take an acting class together at the Berkeley Film Institute, outside the UC system. He wrote *Stacy's Knights.* He continued writing scripts but was tired of it. Kevin told him, "Write a novel. Stop your bitching and just write."

Michael wrote the novel *Dances with Wolves.* He dropped it on my doorstep chapter by chapter. I was reading it, loving it more and more. When I finished, we tried to find a publisher. I spent a lot of time in New York and L.A. trying to find a publisher. I think I had over 30 rejection notices that I later framed for him when it became the biggest selling book in America for a while.

You jumped into that whole New York publishing world— agents, editors? Here comes Jim Wilson, flying in with a book written by his buddy from the bus.

That's basically it. I put on my suit in New York, but I came back with my tail between my legs and no deal. No luck. Literally, we got slammed. I suggested to Kevin that the book would make a great movie: "You've got to play John Dunbar." It took a little while for him to read it, but when he did, he agreed: "Great part." So Kevin and I went to Michael and made a deal for him to adapt his own piece, which is always questionable with a novelist. By then Michael was a dear friend to both of us, and he had written screenplays. He was an obvious first choice. He went to work on the script. Kevin put a lot into the script also, while I was sent off to try to figure out how to make it.

Michael was living at that time in Bisbee, Arizona, washing dishes. He said, "I'm out of here, forget Hollywood. Call me if something happens." I went out in search of a publisher again, but it was easier this time. Once they hear it's going to be a movie, they jump up. We finally found a publisher for Michael's novel. I believe it was Fawcett. The advance was nominal, something like $7,500. So Kevin gave him a call. He told him to come back to town because we were going to make his movie.

Kevin and I went to the studios, but they all passed for various reasons, for obvious ones: Kevin had never directed a feature-length film, the Native American tongue was being used, and we had proposed that no name actors be used. It was something they couldn't grasp.

What happened then was, we ran into a gentleman, Guy East, who ran Majestic Films. He came in along with a friend of his, Jake Eberts. [Eberts] said, "What do you need?" I said, "I need a million bucks up front to do what I got to do: I got to prep this thing, I've got to scout it, I've got to budget it." He said, "You got it." I remember I was in bed in the morning when he called from London. I told Kevin, "I can't believe it, but Jake is on board for a million bucks." So that $1 million started the project. It was real. With Kevin's cachet, Guy decided to do pre-sales. He saw an international market. Europeans like Indians, even Japan was interested. "Maybe Native Americans can sell overseas," he thought. So now we've got momentum, between Jake's money and Majestic coming in and Guy doing international pre-sales.

We planned to re-introduce it to studios. I was filming *Revenge* with Kevin down in Mexico. One weekend I rented some costumes. I put him in his uniform, put him on a horse. He looked good, regal. We said, "Oh my God, that could be a poster." Pre-sales all of a sudden were happening. We finally rallied around with Orion Pictures as our domestic studio partner.

They were the more adventurous ones.
Right, and they knew Kevin. They had already done *Bull Durham* and *No Way Out*. Both were Orion films. Kevin already had a track record with them. Mark Platt was head of production, and Mike Medavoy was head of the company. They green-lit it just before we started to shoot.

We had a budget of around $16.3 million, ambitious for that time. A big decision for me, a tough one, was to do the film split-unions.

That means that I had to be a SAG (Screen Actors Guild) signatory because Kevin was in SAG. I signed with SAG and the DGA (Directors Guild of America), but I didn't sign with the IA (International Alliance of Theatrical Stage Employees). The IA controls the Teamsters, the drivers and the majority of your crew. I wanted to go IA, but I didn't have the money. It was over a 108-day shooting schedule. If you have forty or 50 drivers, the whole crew, the minute you get beyond eight hours, you go time and a half, and double-time beyond 12. It just gets to be too much money. So basically I went to everybody on flats. So I would do that with every category, and we saved, I would guesstimate $8 million.

You have a rare versatility. You are both a hands-on business guy and can deal with union negotiations, but you're also a creative guy. How do you do it, flip personalities?

I don't know if you'd call it "flip personalities," because I hope the personality is pretty consistent. Still, you've definitely got to use separate sides of the brain. The business end comes easier to me. My father was a stockbroker and businessman and understood numbers. I have that gene. On the flip side, my mom is an architect. Personally I always wanted to be more artistic than business. With *Dances* we had to do it on our own, so I handled the business.

The cool thing about *Dances* was that there were so many first-timers in their respective positions. The most I'd ever produced was a quarter-million dollar picture, so now I'm on a $16 million picture. Kevin had never directed before. Michael was essentially a first-time screenwriter, really. We hired a lot of freshmen.

And on location to boot.

Yes, we were out in the middle of nowhere in South Dakota. My first trip into the airport in Pierre, South Dakota: It was, "Wow."

Did you see the Corn Palace?

I missed the Corn Palace but we saw everything else. We had to go there because it was basically where 3,500 buffalo roamed. So the buffalo actually drew us to South Dakota. Kevin and I scouted pretty extensively with our scout, Tim Wilson, and found our numerous locales.

You had to be the producer, but Kevin was the director and actor, so there must have been some tug of wars.

Every day Kevin would always push the envelope in terms of numbers. I would look down on the Indian camp. I would say I think we can do with 100 horses. We'll spread them out, and Kevin would say we need 250. I'd say, "Well, it's difficult where we are, Kevin, to find 250 horses." He would kind of pat me on the back and say, "You'll find them." And I did. Sometimes I might be 20 or 25 shy. I wondered if he was actually counting.

The good news is, he made me a better producer by pushing me. I aimed to please, and I learned it made for better movies. So I realized even though I thought we could get away with 100, it did look better with 250. We had that kind of discussion certainly weekly, if not daily, on the film. I was always trying to say, "Fewer buffalo, fewer horses, fewer extras. Do we need that here?" That was my job. Occasionally, I got a small victory. But most of the time, he pushed it pretty hard.

That is amazing: Two guys who are friends, but who were pitted against each other in their roles. And you came out still friends.

It did work remarkably well. We knew our places. I knew where I belonged in that whole relationship. It was quite amazing. I relied on Kevin to do what he does well, and he did the same for me. That's why the partnership grew. During *Dances*, we heard about "Kevin's-gate," and what a disaster it was. It didn't bother us. One night I thought about it, and said, "How silly is this?"

It was probably good for you to be way off in South Dakota. You didn't have to deal with the suits and industry gossip.

We were out there in the prairie, watching dailies every night. We shot six-day weeks. We shot right into Sunday morning, basically. I'd meet with Kevin every Sunday to talk about Monday's work. There wasn't a break for six months. It wasn't a matter of, "Oh, my god, we need to control the press." You could tell by the dailies that things were working out. I didn't know how good a film it would be, but we could see some pretty cool stuff while we were watching. We had dailies open to the crew, the cast, everybody. I would be lying if I said I knew it would be as successful as it was. I didn't dream as large as Kevin did. He made a big picture. We even talked about the scope of it. Was it going to be 2.5 CinemaScope, widescreen? I'd say, "Kevin, if it's widescreen, we've got to fill the east and the west. We've got to fill the edges on a bigger screen. Why don't we just do 1:85?" He'd say, "No, we're making a big picture." We lucked out and got Dean Semler from Australia to shoot the film. Dean was a big asset with his keen eye. He was very helpful and a wonderful collaborator.

I was struck early on in the film with the humor. Although it was big-canvas, it was not just a somber historical piece.

There is some humor in there. We cast some actors who could handle the comedy. Graham Greene and Robert Pastorelli were exceptional in the funny bits. Both Michael and Kevin always love those comic pieces. Michael always did the set-up nicely and Kevin, as the director, would take it a bit further.

How about post-production?

Obviously, the film's running time was a problem. Kevin's first cut, which I saw at Raleigh Studios, was over five and a half hours. He asked me, "What do you think?" I said, "I have to go to the bathroom." He liked it at that length. He wasn't thinking of releasing it that long but still we cut it before we showed it to Orion. The first screening we showed them was three hours and nine minutes. To get it from five hours-plus down to three hours was some heavy lifting. You did not want to lose story, and the big set pieces needed to be big. Neil Travis cut the movie with Kevin. It was great storytelling. The picture has held up well over time. I'll still hear people say they flip it on at home. They say, "I turned it on, and I just stayed with it. I kind of got hooked with it." That's a good sign to me if you just click in wherever you do, and you just can't turn it off.

So, it was difficult to lock the final reels. Kevin was all about, "We can't shortchange this." The studio would have loved something at two hours and 30 minutes at the most. The problem with exhibitors is, they could only get in a number of screenings a day. So we could have been losing a screening a day with a three-hour-plus movie. I'd say to Kevin, "We could lose a million dollars a day." And he'd say,

"Look, you've got to put out the best product." He stuck by his guns. And the studio, once they saw the movie completed, said, "It works." They left us alone.

Kevin was getting his clout going.

Yes, he was getting his clout. He had done by then *The Untouchables* before we went off to do this. That was his first real payday. With Sean Connery, Paramount—that was a big one. Orion did a nice job marketing the film.

Jake Eberts was helpful in feeling out how to release *Dances*. We actually only opened on 14 screens, platformed it. It came out in November of '90. It did very well the first week. With releasing, there is always the thought: do you jump [expand] it? How do you fill theaters next week? We were never #1 in all the weeks we played the theaters, and in the Oscar run. We ground it out with the best of them.

It's funny when you make a film like *Dances* and it wins awards. And the question is, how are you going to follow this up? What do you come back with? Are you going to come back with another period epic? Are you going to become Merchant-Ivory? Who are you? We had a hundred Native American scripts sent to us, from Geronimo to Wounded Knee.

The next thing we did was about as far away from *Dances* as you could get. We decided to do a love story with Kevin and Whitney Houston.

Tig had a great run going. We signed a deal with Warner Bros. that lasted a decade. It worked very well for ten years for us. So when the script *The Bodyguard* came to us, Kevin and Larry kind of polished it up. Larry hooked up with Kevin on *The Big Chill*, so they were friends, and then *Silverado*. So they had a good working relationship. When the script came up, he said he thought it was a good idea but it needed to be polished, updated, make it contemporary and then introduce it to Whitney.

Kevin really thought Whitney was a great idea, and he pushed for her. For the day it was a properly budgeted film, not huge. They gave us what I needed. When Whitney came into the mix, it happened very quickly. Once the script was polished up, we had Mick Jackson directing the piece and Warner Bros. gave it the go-ahead. That was one of the fastest projects I've ever been associated with: Larry's script, Kevin and Whitney, Mick on board. We shot it right away, and we got it out fast. It was the fastest film I have ever made from start to release. Plus, we shot a lot at one location, at a mansion in Beverly Hills. We kept it simple. For his role as a very square security pro, Kevin cut his own hair [*laughs*]. When Kevin comes in with his own haircut, that's when you know he's getting serious about the movie.

He came in and he definitely supported [casting] Whitney. The studio, Warner Bros., wasn't crazy for that. They had other things in mind. Larry Kasdan had [written the script in the 1970s] with Steve McQueen and Diana Ross [in mind]. Kevin has always been a fan of McQueen's. So, we said, let's stick with that.

The speed with which everyone wanted to get it done helped. Kevin was, "Let's get this film made" and it just got rolling. You have Clive Davis and Arista, Whitney—you have people who know what they are doing on the music end. We had a good music supervisor, Maureen Crowe, whom I worked with. I was the intermediary between Clive and Kevin and Whitney.

You are working with the music world too.

Yeah, you're helping broker a lot of those deals. It was fun, going in. It was like we need 12 songs, and fast. It went out to everybody, the really top people, like David Foster, Carole Bayer Sager, all the great songwriters. Everybody wanted to get on board. Everybody was submitting songs right and left. We had to go quickly because you need that music before you do the picture. That was on the forefront.

Still, you were out front, throwing yourself into foreign territory like you did with publishing.

I talked to Dolly Parton to get "I Will Always Love You." That was a kick. After the film was a big hit, I spoke to her in Vegas and she thanked me for using the piece.

That was your idea to get that song?

No, it was actually submitted to me. Maureen Crowe, the music supervisor, was in place. All the music ideas would funnel through her. We both liked the track. Maureen and I would then take it to Whitney,

Kevin and Mick Jackson. Once we got their approvals, we moved quickly.

That's a tough crowd.

It was a wonderful collaboration because Warner Bros. had a big music division. And you had Arista, Clive Davis, Warner Bros., Whitney, Maureen, so Kevin was in on the choices, Whitney was, I was, Maureen—and we all knew we had to get it done.

There wasn't any backdoor stuff. I don't really remember problems. It was tough to say no to people who had brought a song. There were some very big composers. Some of them were very good, but they just didn't fit.

That film went about as smoothly as can be. Kevin and Whitney hit it off really well. Whitney was great. She knew it was her first really big film, and Kevin was there for her. So they worked out well. It was a good crew. Shot right here in Los Angeles, then on to Fallen Leaf Lake up by Tahoe and finally Miami.

Again, Warner Bros. was right here to back us up if there came any issues. Barry Reardon [president of distribution] knew what theaters to get it in. Terry Semel and Bob Daly were running the studio then. They were the best duo that I ever dealt with. We were there from '91 to 2000. It was a good deal for us. They fed us material. We gave them some stuff. A couple of really good films came through that relationship.

On *The Bodyguard*'s opening Friday, a copy of *USA Today* plopped on my desk. They gave it 0 stars. What did they watch? When I read that review, I said, "Oh my God, we might be in trouble." There were plenty of other reviews that followed that weren't that great. The great news was that on Friday night, Saturday, the theaters were going well. People who came out really enjoyed it.

It got great word-of-mouth. It kept rockin' right on. The music was beautifully timed by Arista—"I Will Always Love You" they put out six weeks before. When the movie opened, it was on the radio. It struck #1 the week we opened. The synergy of that was amazing. When you get a song like that and Whitney promoting the piece, and the studio behind it, you run with it because it's not going to happen often.

I must credit Mick Jackson for his attention to detail. He really was a stickler for detail. I mean, down to putting the piece of paper in the locker, it had to be this way. We could spend two hours on this. He'd say, "The bomb has got to be set just right if it's going to tick."

Again, as a producer you have to push in a certain way.

You are in charge, but you have to realize that these guys are there for a reason, and they're better at it than you are. So, that was a good one-two punch. For Tig to come out and do *Dances with Wolves* followed by *The Bodyguard*, those are two different babies: One in Hollywood, one out of Hollywood; one music, one a period epic. So at that point you say, "We're not sure where we're going to go from here," but that sets you up nicely. It keeps you from getting pigeonholed. Certain filmmakers, you get, "I love him for this, but I don't know about that." That wide combination opened the windows for us. People said, "Those boys can do a wide variety of things."

Well, you have done a wide variety of things from Swing Vote *to* Mr. Brooks.

Mr. Brooks is quite a deviation from *Swing Vote*. You couldn't have a more different type of film. With any film, it all begins with the script. Everything else I do is just to get it made. If you don't have that proper tale to tell, you're in deep trouble. *Brooks* was a pretty big departure, a very intense picture. That was one that initially—I think Kevin felt the same way—that I didn't think that I would want to put that out there, but the writing was so good. Bruce Evans and Ray Gideon had written a great piece of material.

I know a year went by, and we didn't do anything. It sat there. We were reading other material, but we just began to feel that maybe this was something we needed to do. Sometimes you just can't get away from something.

How did that come to you?

Bruce Evans and Ray Gideon wanted Kevin to play Mr. Brooks, So they got directly in touch with Kevin and his assistant, Jasa. She is now head of development. I think it came right through the door. She read it, Kevin read, I read it. Rarely do all the hands go up. Everyone said, "We don't know if we want to have anything to do with it," but we couldn't refute the fact that it was a very well-written piece.

It was a very different role for Costner—a murderer.

Yes, it was different for Kevin, but he took it on. I said, "Kevin, you gotta do this, do that." He said, "I know what I gotta do."

Then you did something completely opposite from it, a Capra-esque comedy. Plus, Swing Vote *had some political satire.*

Yes, there was a lot of satire in there. Actually, some of it went over the audiences' heads. Personally, I think it was one of those films that was shortchanged, maybe the marketing, maybe the release date. It's hard for me to point a finger at anybody when a film doesn't work because it always smarts a bit.

You did 500 Nations.

Jack Leustig wandered into the Tig offices not long after we'd made *Dances* and said, "I have an idea to really do a history that we don't know. Native Americans taken a lot further. I want it to be a documentary. I want it to be long-form, eight hours in all." Kevin was up for it. Jack took on a three-year project. Kevin and I co-executive produced, and he ended up narrating the piece throughout. He was in for the big meetings. I was in for raising the money and helping with the ultimate distribution. But it really was a Jack Leustig production from top to bottom.

How did you raise the money for that one?

Kevin asked, "What's the budget for the piece?" and I said, "Eight million dollars," which at the time was unheard of [for a documentary]. First we need[ed] a network to agree to air it and, better yet, a license fee. I talked to all the networks and CBS, Les Moonves, agreed to air the piece. I remember the fee as about $1.5 million from CBS. They don't pay it upfront but they pay it on delivery.

So I have $1.5 million there, so I turn around and know I have a book coming out of this because not only is it going to become a TV series but we have to have the companion piece. So, I went to New York, and, I believe there's another $1.5–2 million right there. I think it was $2 million.

We now had $3.5 million, so we went to the music side of it. Believe it or not, the music came in. We had a hit with the *Dances* soundtrack with John Barry, so Sony ponied up a pretty good figure for something like this. There was a video component to it too. Warners did the video. Then I approached Microsoft. Microsoft wanted to do it for all the schools, put it on a disc. Microsoft was exploring with new content like this and it was perfect timing. And then my final coup was overseas. Majestic came aboard again, having sold *Dances*; they took on selling it overseas. It was a proper fit for those that had success overseas with our movie.

So I had six or seven partners and by the time we finished the eight hours, which Jack worked on for three years, we got back $9 million. We covered it, plus interest.

So Kevin's clout essentially gave us the money to tell at that time a story that nobody else could. He said, "I'll be the backstop, but you get everything to fall in place." Again, other than being co-executive producers, it is underlying a Jack Leustig production. He had a wonderful group of producers that worked under him and did each show very well. He had his team. The series has traveled overseas, sold overseas. It will keep doing it. It became a basis for a lot of junior high and high schools education about Native Americans. The fun thing, both of my daughters introduced it to their schools. They said, "Hey, Dad, guess what our class is seeing? We're seeing your show this week." That's always fun.

Earlier, what do you learn? You must have seen a lot of things that you'd think, "We don't want to do it that way."

Early on, making *Stacy's Knights* and other films as a director, I learned from my mistakes like you can't believe. When you do that, and you see it didn't work—that impression is forever imprinted in my head. I know not to do that again. I know how to frame better this time. How to cast better this time, how to pick a better location, what I can live without and what I must have. Those things are seared in your head, in a way that is so painful—when you put out a film and think, "This is really cool"—[and] they point out, this, this, this.... I've made enough movies that I've made so many mistakes. As you move along, you learn what doesn't work. I don't go to the theater to seek out bad movies. I will look for certain films that will be inspiring and wonderful movies.

184

I've seen the highs and the lows. You know we made *The Postman*. I still enjoy it. There's some great stuff in the movie, but it got hammered at the box office. It wasn't well received. It was a disappointment. *Wyatt Earp*, for what I do as a producer, is produced as well as I can. The director got everything he needed. We had the budget we needed, we got the actors we wanted, we got a great location, and we built a $6 million set. Everything I could put out on the table, I did.

We had a great team. Our cinematographer was Owen Roizman. The composer was James Newton Howard. Everything was there. As a produced show, I will hold that up scene by scene and say that as a producer, that was my A-game.

What is the part that Jim Wilson really doesn't want to do?

I need to only make "passion projects." I don't feel like laboring so hard for someone else's dream. It's time for me to dream a bit. It's too hard to get up in the early hours, work all day for something you don't love.

It's like you are back at Raleigh Studios in the early '80s with American Twist and producing tennis docs.

Yes, it is. It's like me and *Stacy's Knights*. This is 30 years later. I've done *my Stacy's Knights*, I've won an Oscar, had films that made a lot of money. But there is no green button to press. In fact, the world has changed. I have just finished directing a film titled *50 to 1*. It was very difficult to find financing, and now that it's done, no one wants to release it. So it's up to me. I am raising a few bucks to put it out there. We'll see. But at least it's something I want to do. I like the film. It's a great underdog story. This is America. Buy a horse for $9,500 and go to the Kentucky Derby and knock them dead.

I thought with you calling up investors, they would just want to jump on board. It would be a no-brainer.

No, it's not that way. The funny thing is that we've done over a $1 billion in business with *not* big budgets. Forget video and TV. Even the films like *Swing Vote* and *Mr. Brooks*, which weren't big box office hits, have after-lives. They sell well on DVD. They sell overseas. They are

185

earners for a long time. So sometimes you hit a single. You don't always hit a home run.

Again, you still have the same energy and you want make stories like when you were fresh out of Berkeley and had your 12 × 12 office at Raleigh Studios.

I am the same guy with a few important perks. I have two daughters, and I have been able to see them grow up. That's been wonderful. But, at this age, having worked nearly 40 years beginning with the tennis docs, it's still the story that drives me. I hope I get a chance to tell a few more stories.

Wilson's Filmography

Producer
50 to 1 (2014)
Swing Vote (2008)
Mr. Brooks (2007)
Whirlygirl (2006)
Laffit: All About Winning (documentary, 2006)
Message in a Bottle (1999)
The Postman (1997)
Head Above Water (1996)
Wyatt Earp (1994)
Rapa Nui (1994)
The Bodyguard (1992)

Dances with Wolves (1990)
Smart Alec (1986)

Executive Producer
Stacy's Knights (1983)

Director
50 to 1 (2014)
Whirlygirl (2006)
Laffit: All About Winning (documentary, 2006)
Head Above Water (1996)
Smart Alec (1986)
Stacy's Knights (1983)

Janet Yang

*Janet Yang has a unique and unusual background for a film pro-
ducer. She earned a B.A. from Brown University in Chinese studies and
an MBA from Columbia.*

*Formerly a partner with Oliver Stone at Ixtlan, she recently pro-
duced* Disney High School Musical: China *and* Shanghai Calling, *a
romantic comedy set in China.*

*Fluent in Mandarin, she began her professional career in Beijing
as a translator and editor for the Foreign Languages Press Office, the
publishing arm of the Chinese government. In San Francisco she ran
World Entertainment, which imported and distributed films from Hong
Kong and China. Next she was hired to represent Universal, Paramount
and MGM/UA in brokering the first sales of studio movies to China
since 1949. Yang's activities drew notice, and she was hired by Steven
Spielberg to work on his film* Empire of the Sun.

*Following her production work in China, Yang was asked to become
a production executive at Universal, handling the Amblin account. She
also did the groundwork for* Dragon: The Bruce Lee Story.

*Later, Yang joined Oliver Stone at Ixtlan and began to work in the
independent world. She executive-produced* Zebrahead, *then the urban
drama* South Central. *At Ixtlan, she rose to the ranks of production v.p.
and ultimately president, serving in that post from 1989 to 1996. She
oversaw all development and production for the company.*

Yang executive-produced The Joy Luck Club, *based on Amy Tan's
best-selling novel about the generational discord between Chinese-
American women and their Chinese mothers. She also developed and
produced director Milos Forman's* The People vs. Larry Flynt, *based on*
Hustler *publisher Larry Flynt. Not averse to tackle controversial subject
matter, Yang also served as executive producer on the HBO drama*
Indictment: The McMartin Trial. *She shared an Emmy for Outstanding
Made for Television Movie in 1995 for that acclaimed production.*

Following Ixtlan, Yang partnered with Lisa Henson to create the Manifest Film Company in 1996. Their first film was a joint venture between Manifest and Ixtlan. Released in 1998, Savior *was based on a true story about a mercenary who fights in the Bosnian war.*

Their second film Zero Effect, *inspired by an Arthur Conan Doyle story, starred Bill Pullman and Ben Stiller. In addition, Yang produced Carl Franklin's courtroom thriller* High Crimes *and* The Weight of Water. *Yang's* Dark Matter *with Chinese actor Liu Ye and Meryl Streep, won the Alfred P. Sloan Award at the 2007 Sundance Film Festival. The story was loosely inspired by a true story of a Chinese graduate student who killed four faculty members and one student at the University of Iowa.*

A member of the Academy of Motion Picture Arts and Sciences, Yang is also a member of the Committee of 100 and an advisory board member of Asia Society Southern California. She has been named one of the "50 Most Powerful Women in Hollywood" by The Hollywood Reporter.

Duane Byrge: How would you describe your body of work?

Janet Yang: I don't know if I could link all my films thematically. What I can say is that I never seem to opt for the conventional, safe movie. They all lean toward the edge. What is exciting to me is discovering new voices, or changing people's perceptions, or finding a different way of expressing a story. Surprising or stimulating an audience is what's most exciting to me.

What exactly does a producer do?

A producer is someone who does anything and everything, from soup to nuts, to get a project made. What that *is* changes over time, and changes as a result of circumstances or the people with whom you are working. There are different kinds of producers. I tend to do it all, starting by identifying ideas, or stories through a book or article, or identifying talent. I sometimes have a distinct sense of what I want to make. Sometimes I don't know what it is until it hits me.

How did you start working in China?

I was first living in China in the early '80s. I was struck by how exciting it was to see Asian characters of many dimensions on the big and little screen—it was not something I ever experienced growing up in the United States. I then had this idea to bring some Chinese films out—both so people could get a glimpse of the country, and its emerging talent. Some of these young Chinese filmmakers—like the now-famous Cheng Kaige and Zhang Yimou—were terribly inspiring to me.

Later I was hired to sell American films to China. I then had the privilege to work with Steven Spielberg on *Empire of the Sun.* That was when I got bitten by the production bug. My experience on that film told me what I wanted to do with my life. For a long time, I was the only person in Hollywood who had direct, continuous contact with China. I felt a real sense of mission about my work. But then I realized I also had to learn some concrete skills. So when I was asked to work as an executive at Universal overseeing the Amblin account, I did not hesitate. In retrospect, it was not exactly fair that I got to work on this plum account when there were others far more experienced than I. I

Janet Yang (left) with Amy Tan on the set of *The Joy Luck Club,* 1993. Courtesy Janet Yang.

happened to have the good fortune to spend quality time with Kathy Kennedy when we were in China, where there were very few distractions.

How did the Bruce Lee film come about?

While an executive at Universal, I did have the idea to make a film about Bruce Lee, and sheepishly suggested it in a production meeting. Most of my colleagues groaned, but Tom Pollock, who was running the studio at the time, loved the idea. We then got Bruce Lee's life rights. I gave the project to a producer on the lot, Rob Cohen, who later directed the film. I was no longer at the studio when it was made, but was very gratified by the result.

Overall, life in an office was not for me. I was itching to get back on set, to really dive into projects instead of being involved at arm's length. Producing is great for dilettantes like me—we're "jack of all trades, but master of none." You can have an interest in any number of things, whether it be music or literature or a period of history or visual arts, and whatever it is, there is a way to use it in film.

How did you start working with Oliver Stone?

My boyfriend at the time was making a documentary film in Thailand and was contacted by Oliver to get some information about shooting there for *Year of the Dragon*. We decided to all have dinner in New York. My boyfriend and I arrived separately. When I entered the restaurant, Oliver ran over to say, "I'm making a movie, and you should try out for a part." He had no idea I was one of his dinner companions. Anyway, I started inviting him to events and festivals that I was organizing around Chinese films. And he actually came to them.

While at Universal, I heard Oliver made a first-look deal with another studio. I called him and said, "Oliver, I think you need me to run your company. Somebody's got to."

Bless him, he works from his gut, and he hired me. I think that is why we always got along so well. He is very instinctual. His agents were somewhat dismayed with his decision—there were other people they had lined up for him to meet.

You had the savvy, or perhaps naïveté, to approach someone of his stature.

190

I didn't know any better. I was still very green. When I started with him in '89, I remember asking him what he wanted the strategy for our company to be—what kinds and how many films, and at what budget level, should we be making. And he'd just say, "Ad hoc, ad hoc." He was right! It's actually better than making theoretical decisions, and then not finding the projects.

I had a lot of freedom there because I was not producing Oliver's films *per se*, but instead looking for projects with other directors to produce under our company banner.

*I reviewed one of your first movies at Sundance—*Zebrahead.

I got involved in a couple of independent films right off the bat. *Zebrahead* was the first one. It was the one that got Michael Rappaport discovered. Then I did another indie, *South Central*, which also took place in a black neighborhood. That was not a conscious strategy. Oliver said when he was shooting *Natural Born Killers*, the movie that gave him the most street cred with the prisoners was *South Central*. That movie apparently played again and again in prison as it was highly inspirational to the prisoners.

You were starting out with a range of things, with tough stories. Stories that weren't natural "sells."

Back then you could make them because there were places like Columbia/Tri-Star Home Video, run by Larry Estes. He could green-light a film for $3 million at the snap of his fingers. I look back on this on that time and am amazed. We didn't know how good we had it.

How did Joy Luck Club *come about?*

Never in a million years would that film get made today, at a studio, at that budget. It had no stars, tons of flashbacks and subtitles, a very unconventional story structure with many different characters weaving in and out. While at Universal, Kathy Kennedy took me on a trip to New York to meet publishers. At one meeting, the editor turned to me and told me about a Chinese-American-themed book they had just bought for an amount that was the most they had ever paid for a first-time novelist. And to boot, they only had three unrelated, discrete chapters. They gave them to me and I fell in love. I then contacted Amy

Tan, who started sending me chapters as she was writing them. I had a dream to make the film but had no idea at that point how to go about it. Cut to many years later, after the book became a best seller, and I was working with an 800-pound gorilla, meaning Oliver. I finally had some clout to help get it made.

The emotional impact that both the book and movie have had on several generations now cannot be underestimated. Almost on a daily basis, someone tells me about the healing effect this work has had on their lives. Amy is a rock star! Actually, believe it or not, she does play in a rock band.

What about* The People vs. Larry Flynt? *It must have been a tough sell even then.

It was pretty bold. The writers came to me with the pitch. I just loved it. I asked, "Is it true?" They said, "It's all true." I told them to put it down on paper. I gave the pages to Oliver, and he loved them. We went to Lisa Henson, head of production at Columbia Pictures, and she said, "You guys are the right ones to make this movie."

We decided that Milos Forman was our number-one choice for director. He read it, and fell in love with it. Our first choice to play Larry Flynt was Bill Murray, but we could never get an answer out of him, so our very close second was Woody Harrelson. He accepted on the spot.

For the role of Althea Flynt, Milos narrowed it down to three people. He couldn't decide between Courtney Love and two other women. He went back to the Czech Republic with the three actresses on tape. He even showed them to Vaclav Havel.

That's certainly out of the box, having the president of the Czech Republic weighing in on a casting decision.

How about the fact that Courtney had recently done an interview with *Vanity Fair* where she confessed to being a heroin addict?

How do you get a heroin addict approved for a studio movie?

I went to Columbia and said that Milos would not make the movie without Courtney. The head of business affairs said, "You will never get her insured." I said, "But what if I do get her insured—is she approved?" The executive kept saying, "You will never get her insured."

And I just kept asking the same thing, not knowing of course how I would get her insured. Finally she said, "Okay, if you get her insured, you can have her. But we are not going to pay one cent extra."

All of this was going on right around Christmastime. Everybody was taking off on vacation, and we were going to start pre-production at the beginning of the year. It was insane. I went to the insurance company, and they told us that we would have to pay a $1 million premium. If anything were to happen, they would keep the money. Also, we would have to pay to have a monitor on set all day, every day, to watch Courtney. She would have to take regular urine tests. So now I had to figure out where I would get $1 million. The budget was locked. Sony would not bend on that.

I went back to all the above-the-line people—Milos, Woody, Oliver, the writers Larry and Scott—and I said, "The only way to do this is if we all chip in, knowing we may lose it. But if we believe in her, there's no other way to get it done." Milos agreed first. Then I did. Then Woody, then Oliver, etc. We managed to come up with the million! Milos later told me how grateful he was that I stuck it out. It was very touch-and-go there for a while.

I think people see me as someone who gets the job done, but without having temper tantrums. The most important relationship for a producer is with the director. There must be trust. I try to be a steady and supportive presence for the director because the best films come from a singular vision. The studios may not agree—they often adopt a committee approach, and tend to heavily test movies. So the edges get worn down a bit.

Has there been a learning curve for you?

Of course, but you can't apply what you've learned on one movie to the next one. Yes, there are certain things that prepare you: how to deal with people, how to anticipate problems. But I've never had to get insurance for a self-professed drug addict again for instance.

Would it be different if I had to do it today? The circumstances might be completely different. So producing requires that you are very in-the-moment with what is happening. It's a test of people skills and mental agility. A producer has to be able to look at problems from many different angles.

193

Where does China fit in?

Compared to yesteryear, there is a tornado of activity between Hollywood and China. Even I, who has been in the mix all these years, could not predict we would be where we are today. The box office in China will soon be the #1 in the world! This is historic. And everything is always changing. What has unexpectedly happened in China in the last year is that local Chinese films have done well, in many cases surpassing Hollywood blockbusters. Some of these Chinese films were made for maybe five or ten million dollars. Chinese audiences are suddenly not as enamored of these huge special effects driven movies.

What does the future hold?

The digital revolution is happening as we speak but the new order hasn't yet emerged. China is of course doing its own thing. They are building many new theaters every day. They are cash-rich. There is steep growth.

I often feel frustrated with people's perception of China. These perceptions have become more and more distant from reality. I have taken many people over there for the first time: whether it be filmmaking people or non-filmmaking people. They are always shocked by what they see. Nothing prepares you. I was at a *Fortune* Global Forum earlier this year. Many of their writers were going for the first time, and even they, such well-read individuals, were just blown away by the liveliness and aesthetic and vibrancy. It was not the grim, controlled place they had read about in the media.

The Chinese government has encouraged the movement toward more "soft power." It is a phrase being bandied about in China right now. They know that the world is aware that they are a huge economic and military power but they would really like respect too—in the media, arts and entertainment.

Personally, China has kept me inspired. I enjoy working in a high-growth environment, where innovation is rewarded. This is where I'll be focused for a while again. It's nice to come full circle.

YANG'S FILMOGRAPHY

Producer
One Night Surprise (2013)
Documented (documentary, 2013)
Shanghai Calling (2012)
Disney High School Musical: China (2010)
Dark Matter (2007)
High Crimes (2002)
The Weight of Water (2002)
Savior (1998)
Zero Effect (1998)
The People vs. Larry Flynt (1996)
Killer: A Journal of Murder (1995)
South Central (1992)

Executive Producer
Qi chuan xu xu (2009)
Year of the Fish (2007)
The Joy Luck Club (1993)
Zebrahead (1992)

Index

Numbers in *bold italics* indicate pages with photographs

Index

Index

Index

Index